THE CONTINUOUS VEGETABLE GARDEN

To my mom, Angela Nardozzi. Our Italian roots run deep and she was the rock in our family. She was always there for her vegetarian son, with good home-cooked Italian foods featuring fresh vegetables and herbs.

Quarto.com

First Published in 2026 by Cool Springs Press, an imprint of The Quarto Group, 100 Cummings Center, Suite 265-D, Beverly, MA 01915, USA.
T (978) 282-9590 F (978) 283-2742

EEA Representation, WTS Tax d.o.o.,
Žanova ulica 3, 4000 Kranj, Slovenia.
www.wts-tax.si

Cool Springs Press titles are also available at discount for retail, wholesale, promotional, and bulk purchase. For details, contact the Special Sales Manager by email at specialsales@quarto.com or by mail at The Quarto Group, Attn: Special Sales Manager, 100 Cummings Center, Suite 265-D, Beverly, MA 01915, USA.

ISBN: 978-0-7603-9876-0

Digital edition published in 2026
eISBN: 978-0-7603-9877-7

Library of Congress Cataloging-in-Publication Data is available.

Design, Cover Image, Page Layout, Illustration: Mattie Wells
Photography: Charlie Nardozzi, except:
Alamy: Pages 24, 28, and 77 (right),
JLY Garden: Pages 20 (top left), 45, 52–53, 55, 57–61, 72–73, 81, 86–89, 91 (left), 92 (top), 93 (right), 101, 107 (right), 140, 144 (left), 172, and 185 (left)
Shutterstock: Pages 4 (bottom right), 12, 15, 16, 22–23 (top), 29, 31 (left), 32, 37, 39, 40–41, 43, 46, 48 (middle, bottom), 49 (middle), 50, 56, 64, 66, 68 (right), 69, 75, 77 (left), 78–79, 83–85, 90, 91 (right), 92 (bottom), 96 (top), 97–100, 104 (bottom), 105, 109 (right), 114 (right), 117, 125, 126 (left), 131, 135 (top), 137–139, 141, 165 (right), 167, 168 (right), 170, 171 (right, bottom), 174 (left), 176, 178 (left), 180 (bottom), 181 (right), 182–183, and 185 (right)
Wendy Rowe: Pages 35, 47, 48 (top), 49 (bottom), 54, 74, and 80

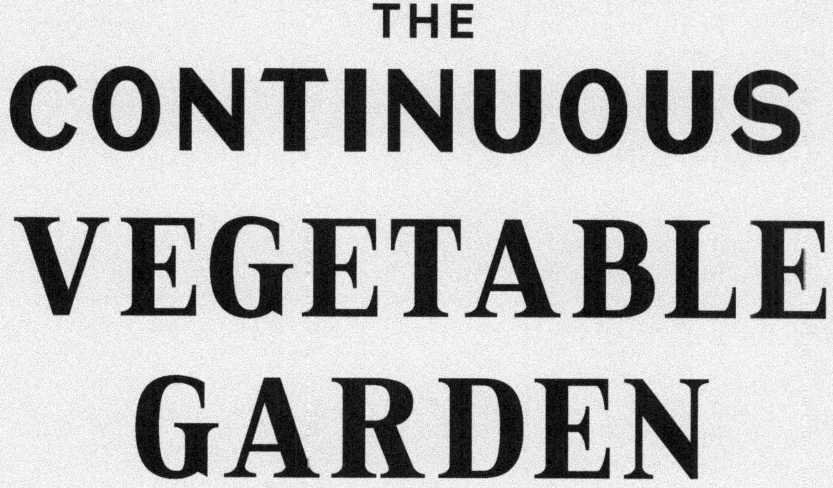

THE CONTINUOUS VEGETABLE GARDEN

CREATE A PERPETUAL FOOD GARDEN THAT SOWS AND GROWS ITSELF

CHARLIE NARDOZZI

CONTENTS

INTRODUCTION

Like most gardeners, my gardening style has evolved over the years. I grew up next to my Italian grandparents' farm in Connecticut. Every time one of their six children got married, my grandparents gave them a piece of land on the farm to build their house. I grew up with all my relatives around me.

Having grown up on a farm, my mom, aunts, and uncles were keen on having vegetable gardens. Every spring my grandfather would till a plot of land for my mom to plant. My brothers and I would help. She would plant a variety of common and Italian vegetables in rows, while we were stuck with weeding and picking out rocks. All summer long, we'd have fresh produce from the garden in waves. First, would come the peas, radishes, and greens, then the bush beans, then cucumbers and zucchinis, then tomatoes, peppers, and root crops. We would eat lots of these vegetables for a while, and then they were done for the season. Between my grandparents' large market garden and my mom's home garden, we were awash in fresh vegetables for five months of the year. Of course, growing up in the 1960s, my mom also wanted to use all the modern conveniences, so she fed us store-bought, canned, and frozen vegetables the other seven months of the year.

When I was able to grow my own vegetable garden as an adult, I followed the same pattern of tilling the soil, planting in rows, and planting vegetables that matured all at once. However, over the next forty years, my vegetable gardening experience changed dramatically. My wife, Wendy, and I have a "vegetable" garden that's chock-full of edible and non-edible plants.

Yup, that's me in my mom's garden!

Most of our garden is in raised beds for reasons I'll talk about in chapter 2. We have berry bushes, fruit trees, native bushes with berries for wildlife, annual and perennial herbs and flowers, flowering vines, flowering bulbs, and, of course, annual, biennial, and perennial vegetables. We follow mostly ecological principles when gardening. We use the no-dig gardening technique and try to always have something growing in our beds to protect and feed the soil microbes. We grow a diversity of plants and varieties and use organic mulches to keep the paths clear and beds weed-free and moist. This has led to a garden with fewer pest problems, less work, less costs, and more fun.

We use a variety of old-fashioned and contemporary techniques to grow our garden. Instead of the "feast or famine" of my earlier gardens, growing too much of one type of vegetable that matured all at once and then having none for the rest of the season, we grow annual vegetables in small batches. We use succession planting and interplanting to stagger the harvest and allow some plants to self-sow.

A continuous vegetable garden will have lots of diverse plants growing.

Interplanting flowers, herbs and vegetables helps keep all the plants healthier.

We grow perennial vegetables and herbs that require less work. We've planted small patches of berries, and we grow a wide variety of dwarf fruit trees to have a continuous fresh fruit harvest from May to November from our garden. We protect plants from weather and pests and extend the growing and harvest seasons with covers. And we even have a wild area for unusual perennial vegetables and herbs.

I have to admit while the raised beds provide structure to our garden, there is a bit of planned chaos too. All of this is designed for one purpose: To have a continuous harvest of food coming from our garden that is grown more in tune with nature, requires less work, and is more interesting, less overwhelming, less costly, and more fun. That's why I wrote this book: To share our successes of growing a continuous vegetable garden in this unique way.

There are some assumptions I'm making in this book. Although we do can and freeze some food, this type of garden is mostly set up for fresh eating. You certainly may can, freeze, store, dry, and preserve extra harvests by expanding the size of your garden space or what you grow.

I also assume you would like to garden more in rhythm with nature, such as allowing some veggies to self-sow, experimenting with edible "weeds," and building healthy soil naturally. I hope you're interested in growing a diversity of vegetables, herbs, and fruits, and that you come with a willingness to experiment with new plants and ideas. I hope you fall in love with this type of gardening and enjoy spending time each day out in the garden doing small tasks like planting, harvesting, moving plants, and enjoying the beautiful bounty you created.

Let's start creating a continuous vegetable garden together.

CHAPTER 1

THE PERKS OF PERPETUAL

Vegetable gardening remains very popular, but for many gardeners, space and time still remain barriers to growing some of their own food. Space has always been an issue with gardening. Yards are getting smaller. There are many competing uses for our green spaces with kids and grandkids playing and families entertaining in the yard. It's no surprise it's hard to find a spot to grow some food.

The average vegetable garden in the United States is about 600 square feet (58 sq m). However, the median size of the vegetable garden is less than 100 square feet (9 sq m). While there certainly are vegetable gardeners with large gardens, 50 percent of the vegetable gardens are only 100 feet (9 sq m) or smaller. In the United Kingdom, the average size is even smaller.

Another limitation is time. In this post-COVID world, many people are back to their "away from home" hectic lifestyles and don't feel they have time to garden. While they may want to grow some of their own food for all the obvious reasons of freshness, food safety, and taste, tending to a large garden just isn't in the cards for many homeowners and renters.

While there is a segment of the population that's interested in homesteading and being more self-sufficient in their food production, I believe most people just want a steady stream of fresh vegetables, herbs, and fruits from their garden all season long. The overall interest in canning, storing, freezing, and drying the excess remains modest.

Plus, modern gardeners want to grow safe and healthy food, not using synthetic chemical pesticides. Interest in growing in ways more in tune with nature and helping pollinators, wildlife, and birds has been steadily rising. I also see more gardeners wanting to have more fun in the garden. They like trying unusual and ethnic foods that require growing unusual vegetables, herbs, and fruits. They want to experiment with using different techniques to save time and money.

What's the solution for a space- and time-starved gardener wanting to grow interesting edibles in a more ecologically friendly way? Continuous vegetable gardening.

Make your garden a pleasurable place to walk in and enjoy the bounty.

WHAT IS CONTINUOUS VEGETABLE GARDENING?

Continuous or perpetual vegetable gardening is a system of growing a wide variety of vegetables, herbs, and fruits so you'll have a constant stream of fresh food from your garden. You'll avoid the "feast or famine" of individual veggies I talked about in the introduction, resulting in a wider variety of foods to eat. You'll be able to extend the growing season and protect plants from pests and adverse weather. This gardening style will help save you money. By growing perennial vegetables, allowing some vegetables and herbs to self-sow and saving some seeds and plants for replanting, you won't necessarily have to replant each vegetable every year.

Because you'll be gardening more intensively in a small space and maximizing the space you have with multiple plantings each year, you'll spend less time gardening. I do want to be clear, though. Perpetual vegetable gardening isn't a no-maintenance technique. Certainly, perennial vegetables and self-sowing vegetables will take less time than growing annual vegetables from scratch each spring. But while you'll spend less time gardening overall, you do have to spend time in the garden regularly to plant, harvest, replant, water, and catch pests before they're a problem. The weekend-warrior form of gardening where you till, add compost, and buy and plant your whole vegetable garden in one day or weekend and then you're done is not what this book is about.

THE JOY OF GARDENING

Since you're interested in creating a continuous vegetable garden, I'm assuming you like the process of gardening. You want to be outdoors in your yard and garden on a regular basis even if it's only for short periods of time. Consistently, gardeners say the reason they garden is to be outdoors in nature and to relieve stress. The continuous vegetable garden is perfect for this type of gardener. It's not about spending a whole day or weekend gardening, although you certainly are welcome to do that. It's more about spending small amounts of time regularly walking, checking the garden, and relaxing. These daily—or every few days—visits will help you stay on top of all the tasks you need to grow a bounty of food and do it in an enjoyable fashion.

EXPANDING WHAT YOU GROW AND HOW

Another assumption is that you like to grow fun, new plants. I suggest growing some different vegetables, fruits, and herbs and their varieties and even some wild edibles. To become a perpetual vegetable gardener, I invite you to expand your vision of what you're growing and when you're growing it. In our garden we love to eat seasonally. That means what's ripe in the garden that day is what we're having for dinner. However, unlike a traditional garden, we avoid planting everything in spring and early summer and a few months later getting inundated with lettuce, beans, cucumbers, zucchinis . . . We've all been subjected to the free giveaways of squash from our neighbors. Maybe you've even been the one giving them away!

In the continuous vegetable garden, we grow small batches of a wide variety of vegetables and herbs. Some mature at different times, but

I'm always amazed at the abundance of food we grow in small spaces.

It's important to have places where you can sit, relax, and enjoy your work.

even those that overlap never become a problem because there just aren't that many of them. Using succession planting, interplanting, and unusual varieties, we grow manageable portions of vegetables and repeat-plant our favorite vegetables for harvesting later in the season. I illustrate different planting schemes in chapter 7 to help you to grow a wider variety of vegetables, fruits, and herbs.

SAVE TIME AND MONEY GARDENING

Saving time is important for most busy gardeners. In the continuous vegetable garden, a special emphasis is put on growing edibles that reduce your workload. Perennial vegetables, self-sowing vegetables, herbs and edible flowers, fruits and wild edibles all work together to provide food with less work compared to growing only typical annual vegetables. Think of the fun you'll have, and the time saved, harvesting asparagus and rhubarb annually in spring, letting arugula and lettuce self-sow in fall for a harvest the following spring, picking nasturtium flowers from self-sown plants for summer salads, and harvesting bowls of blueberries for breakfast from dwarf bushes.

Growing fruits is a particular joy for me in our garden. Once established, they produce a bounty of food with little care. We start by harvesting our honeyberries in late spring and have a variety of bush and tree fruits we harvest all summer in succession until we harvest the last of the persimmons in late fall. By planting just enough fruit plants for our family, we have a constant supply of fresh fruit for breakfasts, pies, cakes, and fruit shakes. I do admit I have favorites. I grow more of some fruits for freezing and making fruit shakes in winter. But that's the flexibility you'll have in a continuous vegetable garden.

Integrating fruit trees and berry bushes into the garden adds another layer of perennial edibles.

Another great aspect of this type of gardening is to save some of your own seeds and plants to save money. By saving seeds, such as lettuce, and plants and bulbs, such as garlic bulbs, you not only save money, but you adapt your varieties, over time, to your growing conditions. Growing plants adapted to your local weather conditions will become more and more important as the climate warms and weather conditions become more erratic and challenging.

GROWING HEALTHIER SOIL

In this book, I offer lots of ideas for growing a wide range of vegetables, herbs, and fruits to make your garden a perpetual farm stand for your family without overwhelming you with too much, all at once. But just as important as the vegetable, herb, and fruit selections and varieties you grow are the techniques for growing them. Many of these gardening techniques are ones you might already use or, at least, have heard of before. But I like to think this continuous vegetable gardening book is a place where I pull them all together. It's not just about different techniques for growing in your raised bed vegetable and herb garden, but it's also about places and ways to grow fruits and wild plants in your yard without taking up too much space.

The soil is where we always should start when talking about our gardens. My favorite technique for protecting and enhancing our soils is no-dig gardening (I even wrote a book on the subject—*The Complete Guide to No-Dig Gardening*). It maximizes the production of your garden, saves space and time and plants grow in a healthier way using nature as a guide. By practicing no-dig gardening, you'll have healthier soil that needs fewer inputs to grow food and helps create a healthier planet. No-dig is a technique that follows the way nature builds soil. By layering organic materials on your bed, and adding compost, you'll have a soil loaded with beneficial microbes to help it with water and nutrient retention. This means healthier soil and plants that require less work to maintain.

FEWER WEEDS AND PESTS

My approach also saves time doing one of the least attractive garden chores: weeding. When you have healthy soil, you can plant closer together, reducing the space for weeds to grow. Mostly that's a good thing, but later in the book, I also highlight how some weeds are delicious. These are the ones you might want to let grow with the intention of harvesting.

Building the soil is something we should start in the garden before we plant anything.

You'll also save time and effort controlling pests. Healthier soils help ward off soil-borne diseases. Plus, by integrating flowers and herbs in with your vegetables, you'll be attracting beneficial insects and pollinators to your garden. What used to be strictly a vegetable garden at our home is now a diverse garden filled with annual and perennial flowers, shrubs, fruits, and herbs. Together they create an ecosystem where pests may still attack, but they're better controlled with help from all the beneficial creatures attracted to the garden. I'll also highlight using barriers and companion planting techniques to control some pests that may still plague your garden. These barriers can also help with the erratic weather by protecting plants from extreme rains, hail, drought, wind, and temperatures.

EXTENDING THE HARVEST

You can also use many of these same barrier materials and techniques to extend your growing season. Chapter 8 offers information about protecting early and late plantings to have vegetables and herbs for an extended period. I particularly focus on planting for fall harvesting. With our changing climate, I've noticed the fall frosts are coming later in our New England USDA Hardiness Zone 5 region. By protecting mature plants in September and October, I often can extend our harvest window a few months.

In chapter 9, I even give the option to bring the perpetual garden indoors in winter in cold climates. Certainly, some gardeners like wrapping up the garden in fall and having some down time. But if you want to extend the season further, I offer techniques to extend your continuous harvest. You can try to overwinter some tender herbs and vegetables, store veggies such as tomatoes and squash into winter, grow herbs in a sunny window, or even grow peppers and greens under grow lights.

The beauty of this book is that I lay out a wide variety of familiar, and maybe less familiar, vegetables, fruits, and herbs, planting schemes, and techniques to try. Pick and choose the plants and techniques you like for your yard. I encourage you to make this garden your own by growing the foods and plants you love in a way that's healthy for the soil, plants, wildlife, and us.

Let's get started with soil building. This will give all your plants the strength and vitality to produce food for years.

Protecting transplants early in their lives is key to getting them off to a good start.

CHAPTER 2

STARTING AT THE GROUND LEVEL AND KEEPING SOIL HEALTHY

While I'm raring to talk about planting a continuous vegetable garden, I want to pause for a moment to discuss soil. The soil is the most important part of any garden. If you can get the soil right, you'll have fewer problems, less work, and healthier plants for the long haul.

I could wax poetic about soils and talk about soil types, textures, pH, nutrient levels, soil compaction, and water drainage for vegetable gardens. But I won't. I'm going to keep this chapter brief and concise. Although this information is important, you can find most of it in any good vegetable gardening book or online resource. I want to have room in this book to focus on the unique aspects of a continuous vegetable garden. So, instead of offering a "Soils 101" class, I'm going to summarize what I do to grow healthy soil. I'll talk about raised beds, ways to create a no-dig garden bed, how to transition your garden to no-dig, how to create soil for annual versus perennial plants, and how to maintain the fertility in your soil as you garden throughout many years.

Elevated raised beds keep some critters away and are easier to work on while standing or sitting.

STARTING WITH RAISED BEDS

Without a doubt, food gardening is easier in raised beds. Not only is it easier on your body, the plants like it better, too. The reasons are obvious: better water drainage, quicker warming of the soil in spring, easier weed control, and less soil compaction. While you can build freestanding raised beds by simply mounding the soil up to plant in, I like to grow in structured raised beds.

Structured raised beds are more permanent than freestanding beds, so while they require more work to build, they require less work once set up. There are a variety of materials you can use to build raised beds. I think the best bed size is 3 to 4 feet wide (91 to 123 cm) and 6 to 8 feet (1.8 to 2.4 m) long. I usually make my beds 10 to 12 inches (25 to 30 cm) tall. This gives me ample room to reach into the raised bed without stepping on the soil and compacting it. The soil depth is perfect for most vegetables and deep enough to kill most weeds and weed seeds in the native soil beneath the bed. You can make square, rectangular, and even curved raised beds depending on the materials you use. You can build the beds even taller or make elevated beds that stand on legs so no bending is required. These tall beds will also deter animal pests such as rabbits and woodchucks.

Tall beds can be as much as 3 to 4 feet (91 to 123 cm) high. Instead of filling them with compost and potting soil, which can be expensive to fill that much volume, create a false bottom in the raised bed. Using marine-grade plywood, drill drainage holes in the plywood and secure it inside the bed, 1 foot (30 cm) below the bed's top edge. Most vegetables, herbs, and flowers only need about 1 foot (30 cm) of soil depth to grow well.

Here are some materials you can use to make a raised bed:

Wood Select rot-resistant woods such as cedar, redwood, and cypress. Softer woods, such as pine, will need to be replaced about every five years. I used 2 inch (5 cm)-thick, rough-cut spruce purchased from a local mill for our beds. The thicker wood lasts longer.

Composite Wood This UV-stabilized wood is made from a variety of materials. It's safe and lasts a long time. Newer types of composite wood hold their color longer and are more attractive.

Metal Metal raised beds are the latest craze. They are made from galvanized steel, corrugated metal, or even stylish, and more expensive, Corten steel. These beds are long lasting and can heat up soils quickly in spring. This can be an issue with cool-soil-loving plants, such as peas, spinach, and arugula, which will bolt or turn bitter quickly in hot temperatures. Instead, I grow mostly heat-loving veggies, such as sweet potatoes, melons, and okra, in metal raised beds. You can purchase metal raised bed kits or modify horse or cattle watering troughs. Simply drill some drainage holes in the bottom of the trough, and you have a ready-made metal raised bed.

Blocks and Stone Cement blocks, bricks, and stone all make excellent raised beds. You can build the walls with freestanding blocks, bricks, or stones, or you can make it more permanent with cement holding them in place. These beds last for many years, are attractive, and can be used to make curved shapes. However, once built, your raised bed will be hard to move. Also, if you use cement to secure your raised bed, be sure to amend the soil well with an acidifying agent if you plan to grow acidic-soil–loving plants such as blueberries.

No-dig beds can be made simply by adding a mix of compost and topsoil.

Metal containers heat up the soil fast and are great for heat loving plants such as melons and sweet potatoes.

Top your no-dig bed in spring with 2 to 3 inches (5 to 7.6 cm) of compost before planting.

Protect your soil by always having plants growing on it or organic mulch covering it.

ADDING SOIL TO THE BEDS

The beauty of raised beds is that you can create your own soil, which is often better quality than your native soil. For example, we have an abundance of clay in our garden's soil. By building raised beds, we can fill the beds with better-quality soil that fosters plant growth while still allowing deep-rooted plants to access the fertility of the clay below.

There are two ways to fill raised beds. The first way is to buy a raised bed soil mix locally that contains compost, topsoil, and other materials. It's important to use locally produced compost because it will contain microorganisms that are suited to your soil and climate. Look for a mix that has a dark brown color, still has signs of the organic materials used to make it, doesn't blow away easily when dry, and has a rich, earthy smell.

While this is the simplest, but also the most expensive, way to start, it's probably a good option if you only have a few small beds. There are many recipes online for making your own raised bed mix. We use a 60:40 ratio of topsoil and compost. You can also save money by making your own compost for the mix.

The second way to fill a raised bed is to build a no-dig bed. This is the method we've transitioned to over the years (again, check out my book *The Complete Guide to No-Dig Gardening*).

Soil is a living entity, and by feeding the billions of bacteria, fungi, protozoa, and other microbes within it with proper food, the soil becomes more fertile and the plants healthier. No-dig gardening minimizes any digging, tilling, or turning of the soil. This leaves the microbial networks that support healthy plant growth intact.

In an undisturbed forest or grassland, leaves and plant materials drop to the ground each fall to decompose. They create a compost layer to feed the microbes, and the soil gets replenished annually. A healthy microbial community is known to create soil that supports better plant growth, improves water drainage and retention, reduces disease problems, sequesters carbon to help mitigate global warming, and even fosters communication between plants.

In our garden, we mimic this process by layering local organic materials to fill a new raised bed. We use locally sourced hay, shredded leaves, grass clippings from our untreated lawn, and chopped-up vegetable and fruit kitchen scraps. Depending on where you live, you can add other local materials such as seaweed and pine needles. Fill a raised bed to the top of the structure by layering these materials like you would make a lasagna, then cap the bed with a layer of compost. If you build such a no-dig bed in the fall, add a 4 to 6 inch (10 to 15 cm)-thick layer of compost. If you build it in spring, add an 8 inch (20 cm)-thick layer. A thicker layer is useful in spring because the organic materials won't have broken down enough to plant in immediately. This technique is cheaper than filling a lot of beds with commercially produced compost and topsoil and is a wonderful way to use local, organic materials that contain microbes compatible with your native soils.

Plant right into the compost layer in spring. The organic materials break down over time, creating a rich soil for vegetables. We find our plants grow stronger, need less watering, and we have very few weeds because any weed seeds from the organic materials are buried and don't germinate.

Another benefit is less disease. Doctor Elaine Ingham is a soil biologist, formerly at Oregon State University, and has been researching soil for decades. She heads up the Soil Food Web School, helping farmers and gardeners build healthier soil. She states the majority of soil disease-causing microbes are anaerobic fungi and bacteria. They thrive in low-oxygen soils mostly caused by poor water drainage. If you have soil loaded with organic matter to help the soil water drain better and provide more space for oxygen, aerobic organisms take over and reduce the incidence of plant diseases.

A no-dig bed looks like a lasagna with layers of different organic materials.

SOIL FOR ANNUAL PLANTS VS. PERENNIAL PLANTS

As you read this book, you'll notice I talk a lot about growing perennial plants in the continuous vegetable garden. Does the way we approach the soil change with the type of plants we're growing? Annual and perennial plants both grow best in well-drained, fertile soils. But there are some differences between the needs of these two groups of plants.

Annual vegetables, herbs, and flowers need soil that has nutrients readily available for growth. This usually means adequate, available nitrogen for these plants to grow fast and mature in one season. Annuals also benefit from rich, loamy, compost-amended soil containing organic materials that are either broken down already or are quick to break down. Untreated grass clippings and finely shredded leaves are good examples of fast decomposing organic materials.

Perennial vegetables, herbs, fruits, and flowers are growing for the long term. Like in a forest, their growth is slower, and they need nutrients that are slowly released over time to support their growth. Compost-amended soil is certainly a plus, but adding slow-to-break-down organic materials, such as wood chips and pine needles, works better for perennial plants. Since some perennials, such as asparagus, can last decades in the garden if properly cared for, proper soil water drainage is important, too. When planting, add partially decomposed compost or mix chopped wood chips into the soil to ensure better water drainage over time. Mulching with these materials each year will help as well.

Wood chips are great in pathways and as mulch around perennials, trees, and shrubs.

CARING FOR A NO-DIG BED

Once established, you'll notice a no-dig bed becomes less work than a traditional raised bed. Because the soil is well drained and fertile, you can plant closer together, maximizing the space needed to grow plants. Use interplanting and succession planting to always have something growing in the bed. This not only increases yields; it's better for the soil.

Soil researchers now know that nutrient transfer between plants and the soil is not a one-way street. They've found plants not only take nutrients from the soil, but they also give nutrients back to it as well. Through photosynthesis, plants produce more food than they need and release some of it into the soil rhizosphere (the area around the root tips) for the soil microbes to use

Mix and match different vegetables in beds based on their growth characteristics.

FIXING A RAISED BED

Use a broad fork to loosen compacted soil before building a no-dig bed.

If you have existing raised beds that are not producing well, have compacted soil, or are weed laden, you can transition them to no-dig. Just follow these steps:

Compacted Soil Soil gets compacted in raised beds due to a lack of organic materials. Just adding compost to the top of beds isn't enough to keep the soil loose and the plant roots growing strong. To break up the compaction, use a broad or iron fork and gently push it into the soil. Rock it back and forth to create holes and spaces in the soil. Don't turn the soil, though. After loosening the soil, add layers of finely chopped leaves, grass, hay, or straw on the bed. Cover with a 4 to 6 inch (10 to 15 cm)-thick layer of compost. Let it sit for a few weeks, then plant. If the bed is already filled to the top with soil, you can remove some of the soil, build no-dig layers with organic materials, and even use some of the soil you removed as one of the layers.

Weedy Beds For weedy beds, consider the types of weeds growing there. For annual weeds that germinate each spring, such as crabgrass, simply remove the top 3 to 4 inches (8 to 10 cm) of soil from the bed and set it aside for another project where it will be deeply buried. This is where most of the annual weed seeds reside.

For deeper-rooted perennial weeds, such as quackgrass, you may have to dig deeper to remove the roots. Don't reuse that soil unless you sift it well to remove all pieces of weed roots. Any roots left behind can (and will!) grow into new plants.

For beds with these perennial weeds, once the soil has been removed and cleaned, add a layer of corrugated cardboard, with all plastic, staples, and labels removed, to the bottom of the bed. Then start layering organic materials as mentioned earlier in the instructions for constructing a new no-dig bed, capping the layers with compost. One of the layers can be soil taken from the bed if it no longer has perennial weed roots in it.

and strengthen their networks. These microbial networks help plants take up nutrients and water. This creates a two-way flow of water and nutrients between the soil and plants, making plants a key partner in soil health.

Because weed seeds are deeply buried in the bed and the soil is never turned, few can germinate. Edible plants are grown close together, so any weeds that do grow often get crowded out by the vegetable plants or are easily removed. In our garden, we do let some weeds, such as lamb's-quarters, amaranth, and purslane, self-sow because we use them as food. I will talk more about these and other self-sowing edible plants in chapter 4. The rich, organic soil created by this layering method drains water well but also holds it better, too. This means less watering when drought strikes the garden.

Chop and drop healthy veggies once they're finished producing to add nutrients and mulch to the soil.

Cover crops, such as oats, will die back in many gardens in winter eliminating the need to till.

MAINTAINING THE NO-DIG BED

The maintenance of a no-dig bed is simple. Try to keep plants growing in the beds from spring through fall or keep the bed covered with organic materials. Each fall, add a layer of organic material, such as hay or chopped leaves, on top of the bed. This protects the soil and microbes over the winter. In spring, add a fresh layer of compost on top and plant.

Another way to add organic materials in fall is to do a technique called "chop and drop." For vegetables that were healthy all summer, take a manual hedge trimmer, chop up the plants into small pieces and leave them on the soil. We've done this with peppers, basil, beans, and many other plants. Diseased plants are cut at the ground level and removed. Remember, don't pull them out and disturb the soil when you're using no-dig techniques. Healthy plants are simply chopped and dropped. This eliminates the need to bring in additional organic materials to cover the beds.

Another way to protect the soil is to grow plants in the beds in fall and leave them until spring. This could be the biennial vegetables I'll introduce in chapter 4 or it could be cover crops. In our New England climate, some cover crops are annuals and others are perennials. Instead of growing a cover crop, such as winter rye, which grows into summer and needs to be turned under in spring to kill it, we grow cover crops that die off naturally. For example, in our garden, we've used a combination of field peas and spring oats. Both plants grow well in fall but die in winter with the cold. They preserve and protect the soil, but in spring, we don't need to till them under. We simply add compost over what's left of the cover crop and plant. Annual ryegrass, buckwheat, barley, and mustard are some cover crops that will die back naturally when winter temperatures drop below 10°F (-12°C).

Now that we are grounded in some creative soil-building techniques and basic ecological gardening principles and ideas, let's put them to use. I'll be referring to these principles throughout the remainder of this book. First, we'll start with growing perennial vegetables and herbs.

CHAPTER 3

PERMANENT PERENNIAL VEGETABLES AND HERBS

When designing a continuous vegetable garden, one of the best places to start is with perennial vegetables and herbs. This includes fruits as well, but I'll cover those in chapter 6.

Most of the vegetables gardeners grow and eat are annuals. This is largely because our agricultural tradition comes from Europe, which features many grains and legumes suited to colder climates. In the tropics, there is a larger variety of perennial vegetables, partly because of the warmer climate and also because of the reliance on roots and starchy vegetables in those regions. This is also due to commercial farming, which favors growing and harvesting a crop in one season to reap the benefits sooner. In fact, there are perennial vegetables, such as some *Brassica*s, which were bred into annual crops to get a quicker harvest.

However, there are still many perennial vegetables and herbs you can grow, even in a cold climate. Most gardeners are familiar with the most common perennial vegetables, such as asparagus and rhubarb, and herbs such as oregano and chives. But there are so many other perennial vegetables and herbs that have been largely ignored in our gardening tradition because of a lack of information or availability.

Before I go further, I should define what I mean by a perennial vegetable. Perennial vegetables are those plants that reliably come back for multiple years without any assistance. Some of our common annual vegetables, such as tomatoes, peppers, and eggplants, are perennials in the tropical climates where they evolved, but they die in most other places where winters are cold, and so we grow them as annuals. I will talk about overwintering plants in this group to get an earlier harvest the following year in chapter 5. In chapter 4, I will also talk about some biennial vegetables, such as beets, which overwinter for just one year, and in chapter 5, we'll cover vegetables, such as garlic, where you save the roots or bulbs to replant. For the rest of this section, when I refer to perennial vegetables, I'm talking about cold-hardy, edible plants that survive the winter and return in the spring for many years.

WHY GROW PERENNIAL VEGETABLES?

Perennial vegetables fill many needs in a continuous vegetable garden. They save time because you plant once and, if cared for properly, you'll have annual harvests for years. They often yield vegetables earlier in the season, when annual or self-sowing vegetables are just getting started. Think of spring harvests of green onions and asparagus as examples of perennial vegetables yielding food when little else is available.

Perennial vegetables are also good for the soil and ecology of your garden. As I mentioned in chapter 2, the best thing we can do for our soil is not disturb it. Perennial vegetables allow the natural soil-building systems to work, creating healthy soil with a dynamic soil microbial network. A healthy soil enhances the plants' ability to take up the nutrients and water when they need it. The roots keep the soil loose and open. The leaves and stems drop and decompose, feeding the microbes that give the soil life. Perennial vegetables also provide habitat for diverse groups of insects and creatures beneficial to the garden.

But perennial vegetables also have a few downsides. Since they're permanent plantings that can last decades, you'll have to dedicate areas long term to these plants in your landscape. Like asparagus, some perennial vegetables take a few years to really start producing. Perennial vegetables and herbs, such as stinging nettle, can spread and become weedy in your garden if not controlled. If you get a disease in your perennial vegetable patch, there's no way to rotate crops to avoid it. Often, you'll have to live with it or start again.

Growing perennial vegetables reduces the need for planting each year and saves you money and work.

Rhubarb is one of the easiest perennial vegetables to grow and it's attractive.

THE BEST PERENNIAL VEGETABLES TO GROW

When looking at the wide variety of perennial vegetables you can grow in a continuous vegetable garden, I consider three criteria when deciding which ones to grow. First, it has to truly be a perennial in your climate. Vegetables that survive a few years then die off aren't tough enough to warrant the label of "perennial."

The second criteria is taste. There are many perennial vegetables I've tried that are edible, but I wouldn't necessarily want to eat them. I remember growing cardoon because I love its relative, globe artichokes. However, even after blanching and boiling the stems, it still didn't have a taste worthy of all that work. I'll stick with globe artichokes, thank you.

I admit this is a subjective criteria, so I suggest, if possible, finding someone who is growing the perennial vegetable you want to try or looking for it in a farmer's market to give it a taste test. Also, grow a test patch to see if you really like eating it before going full bore into the plant.

The final criteria is availability. As I mentioned, many of these perennial vegetables have been ignored in our European-based, agricultural world because they don't fit into the mechanized farming system. So, finding the seeds, roots, and bulbs of some perennial vegetables might be difficult. I do provide some resources at the end of this book to help you source the different perennial vegetables I mention here.

Here are descriptions of how to plant, grow, harvest, and eat some of what I consider to be the most common and best perennial vegetables. I cover perennial herbs and a handful of more unusual perennial vegetables later in this chapter.

ASPARAGUS

Asparagus (*Asparagus officinalis*) is a popular perennial vegetable that hails from the Mediterranean coast. This gives a hint as to why asparagus loves a well-drained soil and sun. Asparagus is a long-lived perennial. I know gardening friends who have grown the same patch for decades. As long as you take care of the asparagus bed and keep it weed-free and occasionally fertilized, it should produce well for years.

PLANT

Plant asparagus in spring. For the quickest production, select one-year-old asparagus crowns from a local garden center, catalog, or online source. Asparagus can grow from seed as well, but it will take longer to get plants large enough to harvest. Select varieties adapted to your area. There are many "all male" varieties on the market. These varieties have been bred to produce few female plants so less energy goes into seed production and more energy goes into spears. Some good "all male" varieties to try include: 'Jersey Knight' (tolerates clay soils), 'Jersey Supreme' (has good disease resistance), and 'Millennium' (better production and disease resistance than older asparagus varieties). 'Mary Washington' is a traditional heirloom variety with male and female plants. For gardeners in the western US, try 'UC 157'. It's more adapted to warmer regions and also has good disease resistance. 'Purple Passion' asparagus has male and female plants and purple spears loaded with anthocyanins. Purple asparagus is not only healthy for you, it's also sweeter than green asparagus varieties. The purple color fades when cooked.

You may also see white asparagus in markets. White asparagus is not a different variety but is produced via a specific growing technique. Asparagus beds are covered with black plastic, or the spears are mounded with soil, to block the light. This naturally blanches the spears. White asparagus is more tender and milder flavored than green asparagus.

It's best to give asparagus its own bed. However, you can interplant strawberries once the bed is established. See more on companion planting in chapter 7. When planting asparagus crowns, dig a 1 foot (30 cm)-deep trench in well-drained, compost-amended soil. Avoid locations that will eventually become shady due to tree and shrub growth. Create small "volcanos" of soil in the bottom of the trench spaced 1 foot (30 cm) apart. Drape the spiderlike roots of the asparagus crowns over the mounds and cover with a few inches (about 8 cm) of soil. Water well. As the asparagus grows, every week or two backfill the trench to slightly cover the spears with more soil until the trench is filled in completely.

Once asparagus starts producing edible-sized spears, if cared for well, it can continue for decades.

Two of my favorite spring perennial veggies: asparagus and rhubarb.

GROW

Asparagus takes two years of growing before you can start harvesting the spears. This will allow the crown to establish and produce more spears for a longer period of time. Keep the asparagus bed weed-free, watered, and fertilized with compost each spring. Allow the spears to grow into ferns starting in early summer and leave them into winter to help feed the root system. Once they turn yellow, you can cut the ferns back and remove them. This is particularly important to remove any red asparagus beetles that will otherwise overwinter in the asparagus bed.

Even all-male varieties will have a few female plants that produce orange-red berries in summer. This is how asparagus can spread around your yard and garden. Weed out seedlings in the asparagus patch or they will overcrowd the bed. You can transplant the seedlings to a nursery bed to grow. We live on a gravel road and since we've been here, I've noticed individual asparagus plants popping up on the side of the road. They love the well-drained gravel and warmth from the road. You can forage for wild asparagus (which tends to have thinner spears) in meadows and fields.

HARVEST AND USE

The spring of year three, you can start harvesting spears that are wider than the diameter of a pencil and 6 inches (15 cm) long. Snap or cut them at ground level and check daily as spears can grow fast. Harvest for one month the first year and then up to two months in subsequent years. Stop harvesting once most of the new spears are thin.

BUNCHING ONION

Bunching onion (*Allium fistulosum*), also known as Welsh or green onion, is an onion type that forms a small bulb, but is harvested mostly for the blanched white stalk and green leaves. When young, they are often called green onions. They aren't from Great Britain, where they're popular, but instead from Asia. They're now grown around the world. 'Evergreen Hardy White' is a common variety. Unlike most other onion types, bunching onions can last for years in your garden, making bigger clumps with each passing season.

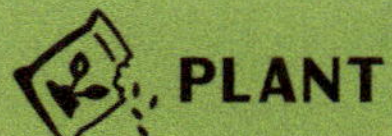

PLANT

Plant seeds of bunching onions in pots indoors 4 to 6 weeks before your last spring frost. Plant the seedlings into the garden after all danger of frost has passed, spacing plants 2 to 4 inches (5 to 10 cm) apart. Plant in compost-amended soil in well-drained beds. Keep well watered and weeded all summer. Onions don't compete well with other plants.

Bunching onions are a spring treat that can easily perennialize in your garden.

GROW

For two years, you won't be harvesting your bunching onions as you let them develop into bunches. By spring of year three, you can dig up the bunch, remove the onions you want to eat and replant the rest. In early spring, mound up soil around the emerging onions to blanch the stems as they grow. This gives you more tender bunching onions for eating and cooking.

In summer, the onions will send up a white flower that is favored by pollinators and beneficial insects. Let the flower fade and set seed. The plants will self-sow and produce even more bunching onions. Thin your bunches annually in spring, to harvest for eating or to replant and spread around the garden. Pop bunching onions around the edges of beds or between long-season plants such as peppers and tomatoes.

HARVEST AND USE

Harvest your bunching onions in spring when the shoots are around 12 inches (30 cm) tall. Separate them from the bunch or cut and use only the green tops. When young, they are good raw in salads. The older, hollow-stemmed leaves are best cooked in soups and other dishes as you'd use onions. The flavor is milder than common bulb onions.

EGYPTIAN ONION

Egyptian onions (*Allium* x *proliferum)* are a cross between the bunching onion (*Allium fistulosum*) and the common bulb onion (*Allium cepa*). It's also called the walking onion or top-set onion. Once you grow this onion, you'll understand why it has these common names. Egyptian onions originated in India but are popular in Europe.

This perennial onion is hardy to -30°F (-34°C) and grows 2 feet (61 cm) tall. In summer, it forms a cluster of small, red-skinned bulblets on top of the large, hollow leaves. Once these bulblets get large and heavy enough, they force the leaf to bend down and touch the ground. Wherever it lands, the bulblets take root. Over time the onion plants appear to be "walking" across your garden bed.

PLANT

Egyptian onions are easy to grow. You can purchase bulbs from a garden center, online, or you can find a friend with plants to share. Simply take some bulblets from their patch in summer, break them apart into individual onions, and plant them 1 inch (3 cm) deep, 4 to 5 inches (10 to 13 cm) apart. Because they spread, we plant our Egyptian onions at the end of a bed and thin them each spring, whether we eat them or not. They also grow as companions under trees or in our wild area.

GROW

Egyptian onions are a low-maintenance perennial vegetable. Leaves can get attacked by thrips, but it's mostly a cosmetic problem. You can dig and divide the plant to make more. In winter, the plant may die back. A good spring chore is to remove any dead growth so new growth can more easily emerge from the bulbs.

HARVEST AND USE

I love Egyptian onions for their early spring growth. I often cut the young green leaves for cooking. The flavor is mild when young. Although the bulblets and bulbs are edible as well, they are very small, so it takes some work to make a meal. The small onion bulbs in a mature clump are spicy.

Egyptian onions form a top set of small bulbs that flop over and root where they drop. It looks like the onion is walking!

GLOBE ARTICHOKE

Globe artichokes (*Cynara cardunculus scolymus*) are thought of in the United States as a California specialty crop. The bulk of artichokes grown in North America originates in coastal California. But this Mediterranean plant is also popular in Europe, especially Italy. This thistlelike perennial produces large, bushy plants that produce a number of flower buds. It's these buds, which are harvested before opening, that we eat as globe artichokes.

PLANT

Globe artichokes are winter hardy down to about 10°F (-12°C). In areas where they're hardy, plant new plants in fall. Globe artichokes form their edible flower buds more readily when the plants have gone through a cool winter. Fall-planted plants will flower the next spring. In colder areas where globe artichokes are not hardy and are treated as annuals, plant them in late spring and hope for flower bud formation in the early summer.

'Imperial Star' is a popular variety for growing in cool regions. It sets flower buds quickly in early summer. 'Green Globe Improved' is a standard variety for warm winter areas. 'Violetta' and 'Purple of Romagna' are Italian heirloom varieties known for their numerous side shoots and small, but very tasty "chokes."

Sow seeds indoors eight weeks before your last frost in cold areas or in midsummer in warm winter areas. In cold areas, transition the transplants outdoors in spring, exposing them to 35°F to 50°F (2°C to 10°C) temperatures for ten days to simulate a false winter. This will initiate flower bud formation later that spring. In warm areas, transplant in fall to overwinter.

Globe artichokes love full sun and well-drained, light soils. Grow plants in compost-amended, raised beds if your soil is heavy. Heavy, cool soil in winter often causes artichoke roots to rot. Plant at the end of a bed to give them room to grow.

Globe artichokes are stately plants making them a great edible landscape plant in your yard. Our plants produce 8 to 10 "chokes" per plant.

GROW

Keep artichoke plants deeply watered, well weeded, and fertilized with compost. Flower buds form in early summer. Artichokes like cool (70°F–80°F [21°C–27°C]), moist summers. Mulch around the plants to keep the soil cool and moist, and new buds forming.

Where they're hardy, they will survive for up to five years, producing new offshoots, or "pups," each spring that can be divided and planted as new plants. In fall, after production stops, cut back plants in regions where winters typically stay above 10°F (-12°C) to 4 inches (10 cm) tall and cover with mulch. In cooler regions, cut the plants down to 6 inches (15 cm) tall, cover them with a thick layer of mulch or baskets, and drape a tarp over it to overwinter the plants. In colder areas, grow globe artichokes in a large container or dig up the crown. Move and store it in a location where the temperatures won't dip much below freezing to overwinter (an attached garage, for example). See more on this technique in chapter 5.

HARVEST AND USE

Harvest the flower buds when they're 3 inches (8 cm) in diameter and the bracts are tightly held to the firm bud. The center bud will be the largest and mature first. Side buds will be smaller and form later. I've harvested up to eight flower buds per plant in our New England garden.

Any buds you don't harvest will open to a beautiful, blue thistle flower. Artichokes are already a stately plant, and the flowers just enhance the edible landscaping attributes of this vegetable.

GOOD KING HENRY SPINACH

Many gardeners love to grow spinach as a spring, and sometimes fall vegetable. Most modern spinach varieties will bolt in the heat or, if they survive the winter, they'll bolt in the spring. But there are some heirloom, spinachlike plants that are perennials, yielding edible leaves annually from the same plant.

Good King Henry spinach (*Chenopodium bonus-henricus*) is actually not in the spinach family. It's in the quinoa family and native to the Alps. The plant grows 2 to 3 feet (61 to 91 cm) tall with a taproot, and it's very hardy down to about -40°F (-40°C). The same plant can last up to five years in the garden. It also readily self-sows. The leaves look spinachlike. Eat the young leaves raw and the older leaves cooked.

Plant seeds of Good King Henry in spring, around the time dandelions are blooming, or in late summer to overwinter. Since this is a perennial green that likes a bit of shade during the hot summer, consider planting it near a deciduous tree or shrub. It will grow strong early in the season then will be shaded by the tree during the summer heat. By fall, it will put on new growth as the tree leaves drop.

Expose seeds to ten weeks of cold in the refrigerator before sowing. Sprinkle the small seeds in pots indoors four weeks before your last frost or sprinkle them directly in the garden on top of the soil in late winter. Do not bury the seeds. Transplant when true leaves form into compost-amended soil. Plant with other greens or in between long-season vegetables such as broccoli and tomatoes.

Keep plants well watered and weeded. Because of their taproot, they don't like to be transplanted. The plants will bolt come summer's heat. Allow the seed to drop in place to create more plants for future harvests. Rabbits and deer don't seem interested in this green.

Good King Henry is a good perennial plant alternative to spinach.

Wait until the second year to start harvesting leaves. Harvest small quantities of young leaves in spring for salads. As leaves age, they are stronger flavored and taste better cooked.

HORSERADISH

Horseradish (*Armoracia rusticana*) is a European perennial vegetable in the mustard family that has been grown for thousands of years. It's called "horse" radish because of the roots' strength. It grows in almost any soil. Most people are familiar with Japanese horseradish, or wasabi, often served with sushi. The European version is easier to purchase and grow and is equally flavorful and pungent. In fact, most "wasabi" found in prepared sushi dishes is actually European horseradish with green food coloring, not true wasabi (which is a completely different species of plant).

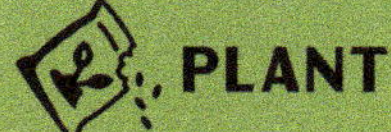

PLANT

Purchase roots of varieties, such as 'Big Top', with good disease resistance and flavor. You can also grow horseradish from root pieces acquired from a friend's plant. Once you plant horseradish, you'll have it forever. Plant in spring in a full- to part-sun location in loose, well-drained, compost-amended soil. Compacted clay and rocky soils can cause deformed roots. Horseradish can spread quickly in a garden, so if you're not sure you'll like the flavor or don't want it to spread, plant the root in a container sunk into the ground to restrict the plant's growth. In the garden, plant the root at a 45-degree angle, 3 inches (8 cm) deep with the thick part of the root pointing up. For a family, one plant is usually enough.

GROW

Horseradish planted in the spring can be harvested in the fall. The large, green, straplike leaves are attractive in the garden, and the white flowers are favorites of pollinators. Horseradish forms two types of roots. The main root grows straight down while side roots grow laterally. Mulch new plantings with hay or straw to prevent weed growth and keep the plant well watered.

The biggest problem with horseradish is its tendency to spread. To keep it contained, grow horseradish in a large container or dig up the whole plant annually, harvesting all of the roots and replanting only one strong root for harvest the next year. In spring, watch for any small plants that grow from root pieces you missed in the fall and weed them out. We grow our horseradish in a "wild" area of our garden where it won't interfere with other plantings and let it roam with some editing.

Horseradish has dark green, attractive leaves and a white flower that pollinators love.

Horseradish roots should be harvested in fall, after a frost, for the best flavor.

HARVEST AND USE

For the best flavor, harvest horseradish roots any time after a frost in the fall, up to just before the ground freezes. Carefully dig the soil away from the main crown of the plant and remove the main and side roots. Any roots left in the ground will sprout new plants.

Save the thickest, straightest, and largest roots for eating. Replant one root that's thick and at least 8 inches (20 cm) long in the hole for next year's plant. Digging and replanting prevents your horseradish roots from becoming too large, woody, and less flavorful.

Peel and grate the harvested roots. The pungent flavor can cause eye tearing, so it's best to process horseradish outdoors or in a well-ventilated location. Add cold water and vinegar to make a sauce that can be stored in the refrigerator for a month. Save roots you aren't going to process immediately in the refrigerator in a black plastic bag for future use.

JERUSALEM ARTICHOKE

The common names of Jerusalem artichokes or sunchokes (*Helianthus tuberosus*) are a bit confusing. This plant is neither from Jerusalem nor is it related to artichokes. Some say the flavor is similar to globe artichokes, so that may be part of the origin of these common names. The Jerusalem reference is harder to track.

Jerusalem artichokes are native to North America and are in the sunflower family. Some believe Italian immigrants saw the flower and called it "girasole," which is Italian for sunflower. The name eventually transformed to Jerusalem in English.

It was grown by Native Americans, but it wasn't a staple crop for them. They mostly harvested Jerusalem artichokes during lean food years as a survival food.

Jerusalem artichoke has sunflower-like flowers that make it a colorful plant in fall.

Jerusalem artichoke plants grow quickly up to 8 feet (2.4 m) tall from underground tubers, producing 2 to 4 inch (5 to 10 cm)-diameter yellow sunflowers late in the season. It's the tubers that are eaten, which are smaller than potatoes and knobby. The flavor can be sweet and nutty, but the tubers do take some work to clean. Newer, named varieties, such as 'White Fuseau' and 'Stampede', have smoother skin, which makes the tubers easier to prepare and tastier.

Plant Jerusalem artichoke tubers in full to part sun in well-drained soil. Jerusalem artichokes are tolerant of sand and clay soils and grow best in a cold climate. In fact, the main problem with Jerusalem artichokes is they can spread and become hard to eradicate. Every tuber left in the ground will sprout a new plant. If the area is tilled, you'll spread them around even more, so it's important to plant Jerusalem artichokes in a location where you're comfortable with them staying for years. I like to put Jerusalem artichokes in a "wild" area with other spreaders such as horseradish and stinging nettle. Cut the tubers into pieces with one to two eyes each and plant them about four inches (10 cm) deep. Jerusalem artichokes make a great screen or hedge plant so consider planting them in a row.

Jerusalem artichoke tubers are dug in fall and have a sweet, nutty flavor.

GROW

Mulch the plants once they emerge with bark mulch or wood chips to reduce weed competition. The plants are relatively pest-free. Rodents may sometimes burrow and eat a few tubers. Cut down the flower stalks in winter.

HARVEST AND USE

Harvest the edible tubers in late summer or fall. The flavor of the tubers is usually sweeter if they're harvested after a few frosts. Either pull up the whole stalk, roots and all, and harvest the tubers or simply harvest as much as you need by digging around the plants. Any tubers left in the ground will sprout new plants the next spring. It's good to leave a few for next year, although you rarely can harvest every tuber.

Clean the tubers and roast, steam, or sauté them to eat. Some people shave the cleaned, raw tubers and use them like water chestnuts in salads and stir-fries. As the tubers age in storage, they produce more starches, and the quality becomes similar to a potato.

PERENNIAL KALE AND BROCCOLI

Most *Brassica* (cabbage family) vegetables we grow in our modern gardens have been bred to be annuals or biennials. But if you dig a little deeper into some of the older varieties, you'll discover there are still some *Brassica* varieties available that retain the original perennial trait. Imagine having one kale plant that stays alive year after year! Let's talk about two of the best perennial *Brassicas*.

Perennial kale (*Brassica oleracea ramosa*) or tree kale is a version of kale that never forms a flower stalk and seeds, staying in a vegetative state for years. Perennial kale is hardy down to about 10°F (-12°C), and possibly 0°F (-18°C) with protection in winter. I've successfully grown perennial kale in our unheated greenhouse with protection. The plant can grow 2 to 4 feet (61 to 122 cm) tall.

Perennial broccoli (*Brassica oleracea)* is also a Mediterranean native. It's hardy to 10°F to 20°F (-12°C to -7°C) and will survive down to 0°F (-18°C) with winter protection. This bushy perennial forms small broccoli florets in spring and then multiple times throughout the summer. It doesn't form the large broccoli crowns we're used to in modern varieties. It's also called "sprouting" broccoli, but be careful with the names. Some gardeners call any small-headed broccoli variety "sprouting," even though it may not be a hardy version. The true sprouting broccolis are older varieties that will live as perennials for years.

PLANT

There are different varieties of perennial kale as plant breeders try to improve and expand the selections of this rare, ancient plant. 'Homesteader's Kaleidoscopic' is a mix of perennial kales that have green, variegated, and purple leaves. 'Purple Paradise' has green leaves and purple stems, similar to 'Red Russian' kale. I've grown 'Kosmic' kale, which has attractive white-and-green–variegated leaves, for a number of years.

There are a number of named varieties of sprouting perennial broccoli that you can purchase as seed. 'Purple Sprouting' is one of the most widely available with small, purple-colored florets fading to green when cooked. 'Red Arrow' is another purple floret variety. 'Nine Star' perennial broccoli is also called a perennial cauliflower. It grows like a broccoli plant, but with yellow, cauliflower-like florets.

Start both perennial kale and perennial broccoli seeds either indoors 4 to 6 weeks before your last frost or directly sown into a garden bed a few weeks before your last frost. You can also purchase transplants of some perennial kale varieties online. Amend the soil with compost and make sure it's well drained. This is particularly important in areas where perennial kale and broccoli are marginally hardy. Space mature plants 2 feet (61 cm) apart in a full- or part-sun location. A perennial kale or perennial broccoli plant makes a great anchor plant in a greens bed, at the end of any bed of vegetables, or even in a flower garden as an edible ornamental.

Kale is a favorite vegetable of many gardeners. Why plant new plants each year when you can grow a perennial version of kale?

Perennial broccoli produces small broccoli heads each spring and throughout the summer.

GROW

Keep young plants well watered and weeded. As with any *Brassica*, watch for slugs and snails on young plants and cabbageworms in summer. To overwinter these plants in marginally hardy areas, mulch the plants and roots heavily with several inches (about 12 cm) of hay or straw. The plant may die back during cold winters, but if the roots survive, the plant will regrow in spring.

HARVEST AND USE

Harvest leaves of perennial kale year-round. Young leaves are best for salads while older leaves are tougher and better cooked. Since it's a perennial, you can harvest into winter and in early spring when little else is available in your garden.

Perennial broccoli florets start forming in late winter. Harvest when the florets are full but before they start opening and get "ricey." More florets will form as new shoots form on the plant. Enjoy perennial broccoli as you would any broccoli variety in salads or soups, steamed and roasted.

RHUBARB

Rhubarb (*Rheum rhabarbarum*) originated in Asia and has been grown for thousands of years as a medicinal and culinary plant. It's most popular in Great Britain and North America, where it is a reliable perennial vegetable that can last for decades in your garden. Rhubarb is an attractive, tropical-looking plant with large leaves and colorful leafstalks (petioles). It makes a nice edible landscape plant as well as a culinary delight. Whereas the leaves themselves can be poisonous, the leafstalks are harvested for eating. They are sour in flavor but are perfect for making pies, breads, sauces, and jams.

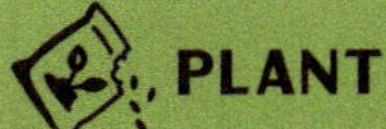

PLANT

Rhubarb is a very hardy perennial vegetable and grows best in areas with a cool summer. Purchase dormant rhubarb crowns or divide a neighbor's or friend's plant to get started. You'll only need one or two plants for your family. Rhubarb plants increase in size over time. Plant in composted manure-amended soil with good water drainage. We noticed a marked improvement in the growth of our rhubarb when we moved it from the ground into a raised bed.

If you'd like the reddest leafstalks, plant varieties such as 'Victoria', 'Crimson Red', and 'MacDonald'. The plants prefer full to part sun. They can grow large, so space them 6 feet (1.8 m) apart and only cover the crowns with a few inches (about 8 cm) of soil. Mulch and keep the plants well watered the first year. Once established, the plants are drought tolerant, but production will suffer. The large leaves shade the soil around the plant warding off weeds.

GROW

Rhubarb needs little attention during the growing season. The biggest keys are to keep the plant harvested and remove any flower stalks that emerge for the best production. Plant stress and certain varieties (i.e., 'Valentine') are more prone to flowering. Let the plant naturally die back in fall. Mulch in winter to prevent root rot and frost heaving.

Divide plants every few years in spring. At first, our one plant grew so large that we had no room to grow anything else in that bed. Now we divide it regularly to keep it in bounds. It's best planted at the end of a bed for that reason.

Rhubarb is a classic perennial vegetable that can grow huge and needs dividing every few years.

HARVEST AND USE

Wait until your rhubarb plants are at least two years old to begin harvesting the leafstalks. Harvest rhubarb leafstalks in spring once they're long enough to eat. Smaller diameter leafstalks tend to be more tender. Gently twist and pull the leafstalks off the plant or cut them off with a knife. Remove the leaves and leave them in the garden as a mulch around the plant. Harvest the leafstalks until early July then let the plant rest until winter.

Store rhubarb leafstalks in perforated bags in the refrigerator for up to four weeks. You can also freeze the chopped leafstalks for making pies and cakes during the winter. The sour flavor of rhubarb pairs well with sweet strawberries, which are also harvested around the same time.

Blanched rhubarb leafstalks are popular in Great Britain. They're milder in flavor and more tender. To blanch your leafstalks, cover the plants in spring before they emerge with a large, black plastic pot or clay pot, sealing any drainage holes to exclude all light. After a few weeks, check beneath the pot and harvest the pale, pink-colored leafstalks once they emerge. Don't harvest all the leafstalks. Leave some for the plant to grow.

SORREL

Sorrel (*Rumex acetosa)* is a perennial leafy green in the buckwheat family. It's native to Europe and Asia, and its name means "sour" in French. Sorrel is hardy to -35°F (-37°C) and one of the first greens to emerge in spring. The lemony-flavored leaves can be eaten raw in spring or cooked as the plant ages. French sorrel (*Rumex scutatus)* has smaller leaves on a lower-growing plant with a less lemony flavor.

To add a little lemony crispness to salads, try adding young sorrel leaves. This perennial green is quick to grow in early spring.

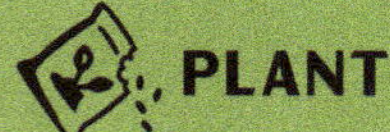

PLANT

Look for green leaf or red-veined leaf varieties of sorrel to grow. The red-veined types are attractive ornamentals as well. Start seeds indoors three weeks before your last frost or sow seeds directly into the garden. Space mature plants 1 foot (30 cm) apart. Plant closer if you are harvesting sorrel as baby greens. Plant in full sun in well-drained soil. If planting in summer, find a spot shaded from the afternoon sun, such as near a larger vegetable. Sorrel is a good perennial to mix in with other spring greens such as arugula and spinach.

GROW

Keep sorrel plants well watered and weeded until established. Eventually, the plants will form flower stalks. To keep the leaves coming, remove the flower stalks when they form. You can also leave a few stalks to mature into seeds and self-sow. In spring, the plant can be divided to provide more plants. Thin self-sown seedlings in spring if you don't want sorrel to spread unchecked.

HARVEST AND USE

Harvest young leaves in spring at any stage. Young leaves are more tender and not as lemony-flavored. Sorrel leaves make a great addition to spring salads. Use older leaves in cooking for soups and stir-fries.

WINE CAP MUSHROOMS

Wine cap mushrooms (*Stropharia rugosoannulata)* are also called "King Stropharia" mushrooms for their large fruits. They look and taste similar to portobello mushrooms. They start out a wine color when they first emerge from their wood chip bed, but they quickly grow large and turn golden. These mushrooms grow easily in wood mulch and they perennialize. For years after the initial bed inoculation, I had wine cap mushrooms popping up in the wood chip mulched rows of our garden, in flower beds, and even along the forest edge.

Wine cap mushrooms are started in wood-chip beds, but can spread around the garden under the right conditions.

 PLANT

One spring I started a batch of wine cap mushrooms in a 4 x 8 foot (122 × 244 cm) bed. You can inoculate beds anytime from spring until fall, but if done in spring, you should get mushrooms by fall. King Stropharia mushrooms can take some light, but I placed the bed in a dappled light location protected by deciduous trees. I put corrugated cardboard under the bed to kill the weeds there and filled the bed with a mix of hardwood chips. I get wood chips delivered to my home by local arborists looking for a place to dump their chips. Often you can get them for free or at a low cost. Using mushroom spawn purchased online, I sprinkled it over the moistened cardboard then added a layer of wood chips. I repeated a second layer, then I covered the bed with straw.

 GROW

Keep the bed watered daily for the first week, then water every other day for the next two weeks. After that, water only when the bed is dry. Because the bed was located in a part-shade area, it didn't dry out quickly.

 HARVEST AND USE

Wine cap mushroom mycelium takes three to six months to fill the bed, then it starts fruiting. Spring-inoculated beds will fruit in late summer or fall, while fall-inoculated beds will fruit the following spring. Harvest the young mushrooms while they're still button shaped and wine-red colored. Cut or gently twist the stem out of the bed to harvest. Keep harvesting daily. They hold well in the refrigerator for one week.

UNUSUAL PERENNIALS AND HERBS

While you may recognize the perennial vegetables and herbs I've described so far in this chapter, I thought to add a few more unusual ones for those who are ready for a little adventure. Some of these perennials might be shockingly familiar since they are common perennial flowers in many gardens. Others may be familiar as weeds you find around your property. Some may be totally new to you.

UNUSUAL PERENNIAL VEGETABLE	ABOUT	PLANT	GROW	HARVEST AND EAT
Wild Leeks/Ramps (*Allium tricoccum*) 	This eastern North America forest native bulb produces large, mild garlic/onion smelling and tasting leaves in spring. It grows in groups under deciduous trees in organic soils.	Often wild harvested, but it's best to purchase ramp seeds and bulbs online. Plant bulbs in spring 3 inches (8 cm) deep and mulched with 2 inches (5 cm) of leaves. Seeds may need two years to germinate.	A shaded, rich, moist, soil with lots of leaf litter is important for their survival. Deciduous trees, such as maple, birch, and poplar, are best but we have some growing under our hickory and oak forest as well.	Start harvesting leaves from bulbs after two years, being careful not to disturb the bulbs. Seed grown plants may take up to seven years to have mature leaves.
Ostrich Fern (*Matteuccia struthiopteris*) 	This stately 3- to 4-foot-tall (1 to 1.2 m) green fern graces forests in cool areas in North America, Europe, and Asia. The edible "fiddlehead" is the young fern that unfurls in spring. It's important to get the proper fern since most ferns have fiddleheads and some are toxic.	Plant nursery-grown plants in a shady area with rich, organic soils. I once grew them on the north side of our house with hostas and they were happy. Ostrich ferns will spread by rhizomes over time as long as they're growing in the right area.	Keep the soil moist but drained. Yellowing or browning ferns is a sign of too much sun, dryness, or too much water. Divide spreading rhizomes in spring to control its growth.	Harvest the fiddleheads in spring when they're still tight in their whorl. Only harvest half of the total fiddleheads on each plant, as they are needed to create the fronds. Fiddleheads have a nutty flavor similar to asparagus and beans.
Sea Kale (*Crambe maritima*) 	This European perennial kale is native to beaches and is salt tolerant making it great for coastal plantings. It grows in sandy or gravelly soils, producing thick kale leaves.	Plant sea kale from transplants in spring in full to part sun. It's important that the soil is very well drained. Growing in sand or gravel is best.	Sea kale can grow to 3 feet (1 m) tall and produces fragrant, white flowers that pollinators love in early summer. While it needs great drainage, it also needs water to grow well. Remove ragged, old growth in spring to encourage the young leaves to form.	The young spring leaves and flowers are edible. They have a thicker texture than regular kale, but the same flavor. Older leaves can be bitter and tough.

All of these plants are edible, but everyone's body is different, so tread cautiously and sample small amounts first when eating them. Instead of gathering these edibles from the wild, I suggest buying plants or roots from a reputable nursery, so you know you're getting the right plant and not harming wild populations.

UNUSUAL PERENNIAL VEGETABLE	ABOUT	PLANT	GROW	HARVEST AND EAT
Daylily (*Hemerocallus* species)	This beautiful perennial is normally grown for its ornamental qualities. But daylily flower buds, opened flowers, and roots are all edible. We grow a patch of the orange tawny daylilies just for eating in our garden.	Daylilies are hardy and tough plants often growing along roadsides and in abandoned fields. For best flowering, plant in full to part sun on fertile soils.	Be sure you plant daylilies and not bulb lilies. Those are poisonous. Daylily plants require little care. The plants can be divided after a few years to spread around.	Eat the flower buds raw as a snack or in soups and salads. The flowers can be stuffed like squash blossoms. The taste is sweet and nutty. The roots can be roasted like potatoes.
Stinging Nettle (*Urtica dioica*)	Despite its name, this herbaceous, perennial green has a delicious flavor and is loaded with vitamins and minerals. Stinging nettle is native around the world. The leaves do sting, causing itching and a rash.	The easiest way to plant stinging nettle is to take divisions from existing plants. Identify the plant properly. Remove small plants on the edge of a mature plant. Stinging nettle grows in part to full sun on moist, rich soils. We often find it on a meadow's edge.	Stinging nettle does spread aggressively by underground roots and is considered invasive in some regions. Plant it where you can control it. Cut back the plant in spring to encourage new growth with better quality leaves. Remove flower heads to prevent self-sowing.	Stinging nettle is best harvested with gloves and a long-sleeved shirt to avoid the stinging. Once blanched or cooked, the sting disappears. While many parts of the plants are edible, harvest the young leaves and stems at the end of branches for best flavor. We make soup, quiche, and pesto from the leaves.
Hosta (*Hosta* species)	Like daylilies, this is a common landscape flower in many gardens. But also like daylilies, it's edible. The new shoots are tasty. It's called *urui* or snow leaf in Japan, where it's a popular vegetable.	Grow hosta in a partly shady area on well-drained, compost rich soil.	Hosta requires little care other than controlling for deer, snails, and slugs and keeping it watered during dry spells. Divide plants every few years to spread them around.	Timing is critical when harvesting hosta leaves for eating. Harvest shoots that are 2- to 4-inches (5 cm to 10 cm) tall and still tightly curled, cutting them off at ground level. Cook them as you would asparagus and enjoy the mildly sweet flavor.

UNUSUAL PERENNIAL VEGETABLE	ABOUT	PLANT	GROW	HARVEST AND EAT
Oca (*Oxalis tuberosa*) and **Mashua** (*Tropaeolum tuberosum*) 	These Andean native, small tubers can be eaten raw or cooked. Oca is grown like a potato and mashua is a type of nasturtium that can trail up to 8 feet (2.4 m). Both need long growing seasons to mature.	Plant these tubers after the danger of frost has passed in full sun. Space tubers 3 feet (60 cm) apart and 2- to 3-inches (5 to 7.6 cm) deep in the soil.	Oca and mashua grow best in well-drained soil and don't like clay. Keep well weeded and watered.	Oca and mashua take a long time to mature, often harvested in mid to late fall after the foliage is killed by a frost. Oca can be sliced and eaten raw on salads or cooked. It doesn't need peeling. The flavor has a slight lemony taste with a crisp texture. Mashua tubers have the spicy taste of nasturtium flowers and leaves.
Yacon (*Smallanthus sonchifolius*) 	Yacon is another Andean tuber; this one is large and grows like a dahlia or sweet potato.	Plant yacon tubers in spring in full sun after the soil warms, similar to when you'd plant sweet potatoes. Plant 2 feet (61 cm) apart.	Keep the soil watered and mulch with organic materials.	Yacon may take six to seven months of frost-free growing to mature. Once the tops die back dig the tuber as you would sweet potatoes. Eat yacon tubers raw or cooked to enjoy the apple, pear, and celery flavors and water chestnut texture.

GROWING PERENNIAL HERBS

Now that you have a sense of some of the perennial vegetables you can grow in your continuous vegetable garden, let's save more time and money by growing some perennial herbs. Many of the herbs I'm going to describe are familiar ones you've previously grown or used in cooking. Let's consider incorporating your favorites into the continuous vegetable garden. Perennial herbs are great for culinary purposes and can be good for the ecology in your garden. Some are good at attracting pollinators and beneficial insects and others are just attractive in the landscape.

Here are profiles of ten of my favorite common and uncommon perennial herbs. Certainly, there are many more you can grow in your continuous vegetable garden. For each, I give recommendations for where in the garden they will grow best. I don't go into too much detail about growing them since that information is readily available online and in herb-growing books.

CHIVES

If I had to select the easiest perennial herb to grow, it would have to be chives. Chives (*Allium schoenoprasum*) are hardy down to -30°F (-34°C) and grow into a manageable 1-foot (30 cm)-tall clump. Chive plants start growing early in the season and continue until a good freeze hits. They also have beautiful purple flowers that bees and beneficial insects love. There are also garlic chives (*A. tuberosum*) with white flowers and a spicier taste. Garlic chives are a good way to add some mild garlic flavor to recipes. I find garlic chives are not as robust as common chives.

Chives have slightly oniony-flavored leaves. The purple flowers are edible too.

SITE

Chives are good herbs to grow on the corner of a bed or around other perennial vegetables, such as kale, since it tolerates some shade. The plants stay in a clump form, so they don't compete with other vegetables or herbs. They also are great in containers.

PLANT

Chives are easy to grow from seed or division from a friend's plant. They thrive in full to part sun in well-drained, moist soil. Space plants 1 to 2 feet (30 to 61 cm) apart.

GROW

Clumps of this allium family perennial slowly expand with time and can be divided in spring as needed. Once the flowers fade, cut back the whole plant so it regrows more tender, new growth. You can do this a few times during the growing season. Chives do self-sow, so either move young seedlings or weed them out in the spring.

HARVEST AND USE

Enjoy the young greens early in the season on salads, potatoes, and eggs. The flowers are edible as well. Consider bringing a potted chive plant indoors to a sunny window to enjoy fresh chives in winter. See more on growing perennials in containers on page 63.

FENNEL

With my Italian roots, the anise-flavored fennel was a staple in my mom's kitchen growing up. She would chop up raw fennel bulbs and lightly dress them with olive oil, balsamic vinegar, salt, and pepper. It was a spring treat in our house. There are two types of fennel: bulb Florence fennel (*Foeniculum vulgare azoricum*) and leaf fennel (*F. vulgare*). The leaf fennel is hardy to -30°F (-34°C). While most leaf fennel has green leaves, 'Bronze' fennel is a dark red-leaved variety. Bulb Florence fennel is less hardy and a biennial that flowers, sets seed, then dies over two years. However, we've had it self-sow in our garden to give us a continual crop of plants. Varieties such as 'Preludio', 'Fino', and 'Dragon' are good ones to grow.

Bulb fennel has a strong anise flavor and it's great eaten raw with olive oil, balsamic vinegar, salt, and pepper.

SITE

Grow bulb fennel in spring as a succession plant since it's harvested in early summer. Let a few plants go to seed to form a tall plant in your wild area. Leaf fennel grows 2 to 3 feet (61 to 91 cm) tall and produces sweet-tasting ferns and seeds but not a bulb. It's best grown in a wild area or at the back of a bed.

PLANT

Start fennel seeds indoors three weeks before your last frost date and transplant them 8 inches (20 cm) apart into the garden after all danger of frost has passed. Plant both leaf and bulb fennels in a sunny, well-drained location in compost-rich soil.

GROW

Keep weeds controlled and keep fennel well watered. Grow fennel early in the season since Florence fennel needs cool weather to form a bulb. The stalks can be 6 feet (1.8 m) tall with yellow flowers. Fennel has few pests and is a food source for certain butterfly larvae.

HARVEST AND USE

Harvest Florence fennel when the bulb reaches 3 inches (8 cm) in diameter. You'll sacrifice the whole plant to harvest. Harvest individual leaf fennel leaves and stalks as needed throughout the summer to garnish savory dishes. Raw fennel seeds are a digestive aid.

LAVENDER

Lavender (*Lavandula* spp.) is one of those multi-faceted plants that can be used in food, tea, perfumes, lotions, potpourris, sachets, and in dried flower arrangements. The hardiest are the English lavender varieties such as 'Munstead' and 'Hidcote', which survive winter temperatures down to -20°F (-29°C). *Lavandula* hybrids, such as 'Phenomenal', are hardy to -20°F (-29°C) and very productive. French lavender and Spanish lavender (*L. stoechas*) have a stronger scent in the flowers and leaves, but are only hardy to about 10°F (-12°C).

Lavender plants are beautiful and the flowers have many culinary and cosmetic uses.

SITE

Lavender plants can grow 1 to 3 feet (30 to 91 cm) tall and wide and are best planted in the front or corner of a bed or with other Mediterranean flowers and herbs. In the continuous vegetable garden, they're great at attracting beneficial insects.

GROW

Lavender plants are relatively care-free. Add compost around the plants in spring. Cut back established plants in spring by one-third to stimulate new growth. The new growth has better fragrance and produces better flowers. Cut the flowers for drying and crafting once they are mature. In cold areas, mulch lavender plants with wood chips in late fall. Bury the plant with a 1-foot (30 cm)-deep mound to protect the crown.

PLANT

Lavender likes a well-drained soil and lots of sun. Find the sunniest location for this plant and make sure the soil dries out between waterings. Planting near other full sun-loving herbs and vegetables, such as basil and peppers, is best. Although you can start plants from seed, it's easiest to buy transplants. You can also easily start this plant from cuttings taken from a friend's plant. If properly cared for, lavender can last for years in your garden.

HARVEST AND USE

Collect flowers when they open in the morning for the best fragrance. Dry them in a well-ventilated warm room. Harvest stems with leaves as needed for cooking and crafts. Use lavender in salads, soups, cookies, and cakes.

LEMON BALM

Lemon is a common scent and flavor in herbs. Lemon thyme, lemon basil, and lemon verbena all have this delightful fragrance. But lemon balm (*Melissa officinalis*) is my favorite.

First, be warned, lemon balm can be a brute in the garden. Lemon balm grows quickly into a 2 to 3-foot (61 to 91 cm)-tall herb that spreads primarily by seeds and an ever-expanding clump. The leaves are loaded with scent and flavor, and one plant is all you'll ever need. The white flowers are favorites of bees and beneficial insects.

SITE

While lemon balm is in the mint family, it doesn't spread by rhizomes as aggressively as mint. However, it self-sows readily, and the clump expands quickly. Because of lemon balm's penchant to spread, weed out seedlings in spring, deadhead flower stalks to prevent seed drop, or grow sterile varieties such as 'Compacta' or variegated varieties such as 'All Gold', which won't set prolific seed. Plant lemon balm among other spreading herbs, such as mint, to keep it under control.

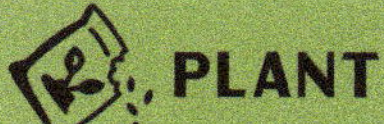

PLANT

Like mint, lemon balm grows best in full sun but will tolerate part shade. It thrives in raised beds in well-drained soil. Lemon balm grows easily from seeds, transplants, or divisions from existing plants. Divisions from a friend's plant is probably the easiest way to get started.

GROW

Feed lemon balm compost each spring. The plant is hardy to -20°F (-29°C). We protect it from harsh winters by piling on the wood chips in late fall. Even if the top dies back to the ground, the roots will resprout and give you plenty of lemon balm for summer. Divide lemon balm plants in spring to keep it under control and to share. Cut back the plant in spring and periodically in summer to promote more new growth, better-quality leaves, and to keep it from enlarging too quickly.

HARVEST AND USE

Harvest stems and leaves as needed for use in soups, summer lemonade, tea, and salads.

Lemon balm has lemony-flavored leaves that are great in recipes and drinks.

LOVAGE

When I first grew lovage (*Levisticum officinale*), I didn't realize what I was getting into. This perennial herb can grow huge (up to 6 feet [1.8 m]) in one season and provide more than enough leaves and stems for cooking. The leaves look like celery leaves and the flavor is celery-like with a sweet anise tone to it. It's a great perennial herb for the chilly North since it's hardy to -40°F (-40°C). The plant dies back to the roots in most areas in fall but emerges quickly in spring to grow into its statuesque form. The flowers are not significant, but they are good for pollinators.

Lovage has a celery-like flavor but is much easier to grow than celery itself.

SITE

Because it grows so vertically, plant lovage on the end of a bed similar to how you'd grow rhubarb. You'll only need one plant unless you become a lovage fanatic.

PLANT

Lovage can be grown from seed or divisions. Start seed six to eight weeks before the last frost and transplant seedlings into the garden spaced 2 feet (61 cm) apart. Plant in full sun in well-drained soil.

GROW

Keep lovage's soil evenly moist and feed the plants with compost in spring and compost tea in summer. If lovage dries out, the flavor can turn bitter. Lovage can take care of itself in the garden and has few problems with weeds and pests.

HARVEST AND USE

Harvest just leaves the first year until the plant gets settled. After that, harvest whole stalks for use in soups, stews, and salads. In England, they make a winter tonic and brandy from lovage.

MINT

I could write a book on mint (*Mentha* spp.), the different varieties, and their uses in the kitchen and yard. But I'll keep my comments to the point for this book.

As you may know, mint can aggressively spread by rhizomes depending on the type you're growing. Peppermint and spearmint can be brutes in the garden, but variegated pineapple mint and banana mint are a bit tamer. Peppermint has the highest menthol content and strongest flavor. There are also mints with hints of lemon, lime, orange, and even chocolate flavors. Most mints are hardy to -20°F (-29°C). Some specialty mints are more tender.

Mint is best grown in containers or in the garden where it can be stopped from spreading.

SITE

It's important to plant mint where you don't mind it spreading or where it can be naturally contained. We grow peppermint and spearmint under our trees in our lawn and in our hedgerow of deciduous shrubs. The mint spreads, forming a thick mat that blocks other weeds from growing. Even if it escapes into the lawn, I love the smell when I mow.

In the garden, you'll have to grow less aggressive varieties or plant it in a container that's buried in the ground to slow down the spreading rhizomes. Planting mint near a wall, foundation, or in a deep shade area will slow its spread as well. It's also great in a container on a deck or patio.

PLANT

While you can start mint from seed, it's probably easiest to get a division from a friend's garden. If you're looking for unusual varieties, try online sources or local garden centers. Mint grows best in full to part sun in a wide range of soils as long as it stays moist. Ours grows fine in clay, so drainage isn't as important as it is with other perennial herbs.

GROW

Mint has few needs. We rarely fertilize or water it. Once established, it will spread. Divide it annually in spring to keep it in bounds. Mint also flowers and is an attractive perennial herb to grow to support pollinators and beneficial insects.

HARVEST AND USE

Harvest mint stems and leaves as needed any time during the summer. Mint is great in teas, and with food such as lamb, fish, peas, and potatoes.

OREGANO

My Italian mom used to love to cook with oregano. The distinct fragrance of Greek oregano (*Origanum vulgare hirtum*) permeated her tomato sauces, soups, pizzas, and pasta dishes. This perennial herb is a great one in a continuous vegetable garden. It's easy to grow, hardy to -30°F (-34°C) once established, and produces loads of fragrant, fresh leaves from spring to fall. Because it's low growing and spreading, it's a great understory plant in the garden as long as it gets enough sun.

Oregano is a great ground cover plant, pollinator favorite, and great addition to sauces and soups.

SITE

We grow oregano close to the kitchen for cooking. It pals around with thyme, and the two herbs make a nice ground cover together. In the garden, you can grow it on the edge of a bed with other Mediterranean climate-loving plants, such as eggplant and peppers. It will cascade over the edge, not taking up much room, while still receiving the light it needs.

PLANT

Plant oregano from seed or divisions. Sow seeds indoors six to eight weeks before transplanting. Sow on the top of potting soil that is kept evenly moist. It can take up to three weeks for seeds to germinate. You can also take divisions from a friend's plant or stems cuttings anytime during the growing season. Plant in full sun in very well drained soil. Oregano needs good water drainage to survive the winter.

GROW

Oregano will spread a few feet and grow 1 to 2 feet (30 to 61 cm) tall. Cut back overwintering plants in spring to stimulate new growth and better-quality leaves. Cutting stems in summer keeps the new growth coming. Oregano likes it on the dry side, so only water if it's very dry. Oregano needs little soil fertility.

HARVEST AND USE

Harvest stems with young leaves for cooking. Young leaves have the best fragrance and taste, especially right before flowering. Harvest in the morning. Select stems in summer for drying oregano for winter use. Although the white to pale pink flowers are popular with pollinators, they decrease quality leaf production. Remove the flower buds from some plants for better leaf production but leave some to flower for the insects.

ROSEMARY

Rosemary (*Salvia rosmarinus*) is a great annual herb in cold climates, unless brought indoors for winter, and a perennial landscape plant and herb in warmer climates. This woody plant is a shrub, and, if you are gardening in an area where winters don't dip below 10°F to 20°F (-12°C to -7°C), it's a perennial landscape plant with aromatic, spiky leaves and blue or white flowers. It's also a great culinary plant. I bring a pot indoors each year from our garden to overwinter.

There are a number of varieties of rosemary to grow. 'Arp' is one of the most cold-tolerant varieties, surviving down to about -10°F (-23°C). 'Tuscan Blue' is known for its aromatic leaves and beautiful flowers. 'Barbeque' is known for its strong, fragrant stems for grilling, and 'Prostrate' is a cascading variety that hugs the ground as it grows.

GROW

Since rosemary has woody stems, prune established plants in spring to stimulate new growth, which is more fragrant and flavorful. Water only when very dry. Plant where there is good airflow to prevent powdery mildew disease. Allow some plants to flower to attract pollinators and other insects. Protect plants in marginally hardy areas with a pile of wood chips over the base of the plant in late fall. Grow containers indoors in winter by placing them in a sunny window, protected from cold drafts, with good airflow around the plant. Keep the soil barely moist.

Grow rosemary in pots or in the ground. In warmer climates, this herb gets so large it turns into a shrub.

SITE

Grow rosemary in warm climate gardens as a shrub in the landscape. It can grow in raised beds to take advantage of the well-drained soil, or around the house as an edible ornamental. In colder climates, grow rosemary with other Mediterranean herbs and plants in the garden or in a container to be moved indoors for winter.

PLANT

Rosemary is difficult to germinate from seed, so it's best to purchase transplants locally or through online sources. Plant in full sun in very well-drained soil. Poorly drained, clay soils are a death knell for rosemary. Plant it in containers to keep plants close to the kitchen.

HARVEST AND USE

Harvest stems starting in spring and throughout the growing season. Harvesting whole stems, even if you don't need all the leaves, keeps the shrub looking attractive. Dry leaves for winter use.

SAGE

Common sage (*Salvia officinalis*) is a hardy, versatile plant for your garden, surviving winter temperatures down to about -20°F (-29°C). There are also many other sage types such as clary sage and pineapple sage, but common sage is the most common edible sage. This member of the mint family is perennial and has broad, evergreen leaves that can be green or variegated. The plants stand 1 to 2 feet (30 to 61 cm) tall and make a beautiful edible landscape herb as well as a culinary one. Beside the green-leaved varieties, there are color variations including 'Icterina' with green-and-gold leaves and 'Tricolor' with yellow, mauve, and green leaves.

SITE

Sage is a beautiful plant, so it should be planted where it can be appreciated and easily harvested. Sage pairs well with other Mediterranean herbs, such as lavender and rosemary, looks fabulous in a mixed container with other herbs or leafy greens, and is a showpiece at the end of a raised bed garden.

Sage is a Mediterranean herb that thrives in full sun on well-drained soil.

PLANT

Plant sage from seed or transplants from a garden center or purchased online. While you might only need one or two plants for harvesting leaves, it's such a pretty plant that it's nice to incorporate more into the garden. Plant in a full-sun location in well-drained soil. Space plants 2 feet (61 cm) apart.

GROW

Sage grows best during the cool conditions of spring and fall. Give sage some shade in warmer climates in midsummer. Keep well watered, especially the first year. Let plants get established the first year by not pruning. In subsequent years, prune sage hard in spring to create a good branch structure and stimulate new growth. This also reduces powdery mildew disease, which occurs when the plants are thick with leaves. After about five years, the plant may get too woody, and it may be time to start a new one. You can start new plants by rooting stem cuttings in spring.

HARVEST AND USE

Harvest sparingly the first year. Starting the second year, remove whole stems as needed during the growing season for eating. Stop pruning two months before a fall freeze. Use sage in a variety of recipes, including with meat, beans, soups, and salads.

THYME

Common thyme (*Thymus vulgaris*) is another beautiful culinary herb. It forms a 6 to 12 inch (15 to 30 cm)-tall mound. There are selections that are just grown as ornamentals, such as creeping thyme (*T. serpyllum*), and others that offer a unique scent and taste, such as golden lemon thyme (*T. citriodorus*). Common thyme is hardy down to -20°F (-29°C) and creeps along the ground, making it a perfect edge-of-a-flower-border plant. It also can cascade off a raised bed or over a container's edge. Thyme flowers are favorites of bees and pollinators, and they're attractive.

Thyme is another low-growing culinary herb that looks as good as the leaves taste.

SITE

Thyme pairs well with oregano as two low-growing herbs in the garden. They grow best at the edge of raised beds where they can get the most light, between larger herb or vegetable plants as long as they get enough sun, and in containers.

GROW

Keep thyme plants well watered until established. Amend the soil with compost in spring. To keep thyme from getting woody and less productive, regularly harvest. If it gets out of control, prune it hard in late winter. Harvesting and pruning stimulates new growth, which produces better-quality leaves for cooking. In marginally hardy areas, protect thyme plants in late fall with a light covering of wood chips around the root zone.

PLANT

While you can start thyme from seed, the seed is very small and takes up to one month to germinate. It's easier to purchase seedlings or take cuttings from a friend's plant. You can root 4 to 6 inch (10 to 15 cm)-long stem cuttings in spring. Remove the lower leaves, dip the cut end in rooting hormone powder, and stick the base of the cuttings in a pot filled with moistened potting soil.

Plant thyme in full sun. Good water drainage is key to thyme overwintering.

HARVEST AND USE

Harvest thyme stems sparingly the first year. After that, harvest individual stems just before the plant flowers for best quality and flavor. Use thyme to flavor vinegars and oils and add to stews, soups, egg dishes, bean dishes, and sauces. Use lemon-flavored varieties in teas or in any dish calling for a lemony zing.

CHART OF PLACES TO GROW PERENNIAL VEGETABLES AND HERBS

PERENNIAL VEGETABLES AND HERBS	STAND ALONE	RAISED BED EDGE/CORNER	INTER-PLANTING	GROUND COVER	WILD AREA
Asparagus	✓				
Bunching onion		✓	✓		
Chives		✓	✓		
Egyptian onion		✓	✓		✓
Fennel	✓	✓			✓
Globe artichoke	✓	✓			
Good King Henry spinach			✓		
Horseradish		✓			✓
Jerusalem artichoke	✓				✓
Lavender		✓	✓	✓	
Lemon balm	✓	✓			
Lovage	✓				
Mint			✓	✓	✓
Oregano		✓	✓	✓	
Perennial broccoli	✓	✓			
Perennial kale	✓	✓			
Rhubarb	✓	✓			
Rosemary	✓	✓	✓		
Sage	✓	✓	✓		
Sorrel			✓	✓	
Thyme		✓	✓	✓	
Wine cap mushrooms	✓		✓		

KEY:

Stand Alone: These plants are large and can take over a space. Provide enough space for them by planting in areas where they won't shade other plants.

Raised Bed/Corner Edge: These plants also can be large, so they need to be at the end of a bed to not interfere with the growth of other plants. They also can be clump-forming plants so they're easier to manage or can cascade over the bed's edge.

Interplanted: These plants are low growing and can grow around larger plants as long as they get enough sun. Many perennial herbs can be interplanted.

Ground Cover: These plants can spread by creeping and are good ground covers around larger plants as long as the larger plants are well established and they get enough sun.

Wild Area: These plants need room to spread on their own and don't mind competition from other spreading plants.

GROWING PERENNIAL VEGETABLES AND HERBS IN CONTAINERS

It's great to grow perennial vegetables and herbs in your garden and raised beds, but what if you don't have enough room for either method? Also, what about perennial vegetables and herbs that like to spread? There's nothing worse than having a perennial, such as mint, take over a whole bed. One option is to grow perennials in containers. Container gardening provides more room for more plants in a space-starved garden and keeps aggressive plants in check.

Consider growing your herbs and vegetables together such as this beautiful container of Swiss chard and tricolor sage.

THE BEST PERENNIAL VEGETABLES AND HERBS FOR CONTAINERS

There are two options when planting a perennial container vegetable or herb garden. You can plant one type of perennial in each pot or plant multiple perennials per container. The "one pot, one plant" method is good for large perennials and those that like to spread aggressively. These include plants such as those in the mint family (i.e., mint, lemon balm, oregano), tarragon, horseradish, rhubarb, Egyptian onions, and artichokes.

When it comes to planting multiple perennials in a single container, mixing and matching perennial vegetables and herbs together can be a fun way to grow a variety of plants without taking up too much space. Match perennial vegetables and herbs with similar sun, soil, water, and growth needs together. A few good examples are a Mediterranean herb pot with any combination of herbs from this region, such as thyme, lavender, rosemary, sage, and marjoram. An allium family pot of Egyptian onions and chives could be fun to grow. Rosemary and chamomile are also good choices as they share similar care needs. You can even grow a self-sowing pot by creating a collection of plants that self-sow, such as dill, cilantro, and parsley. Although they are not true perennials, these plants self-sow rampantly and you'll be able to recreate the pot each spring from new seedlings that pop up from dropped seeds.

CONTAINERS AND SOILS FOR GROWING PERENNIALS IN POTS

One of the first considerations for planting perennials in containers is the container itself. In general, the bigger, the better for containers. Larger pots give you more options and allow aggressive plants to thrive in the container longer. Of course, part of the consideration for container growing is the space you have and the ability to move larger containers for proper sun exposure and winter protection if needed.

Perennial vegetables and herbs can be grown in containers even in the North. They will just need some winter protection.

It's best to start with containers that are 14 to 16 inches (36 to 41 cm) in diameter with good drainage holes to accommodate large perennials and offer options for multiple plants. The smaller the pot, the more often you'll need to repot or divide the plants to keep them the right size for their container.

Next, you'll want to match the potting soil with the type of plants you're growing. For perennials that love well-drained soil, such as any of the Mediterranean herbs, use a light potting soil mix that has plenty of perlite for water drainage. Perennials that like a wetter or denser soil, such as parsley and mint, might benefit from some compost being added to the potting mix.

CARE FOR CONTAINER PERENNIAL VEGETABLES AND HERBS

Plant full-sun–loving perennial vegetables and herbs, including artichoke, lavender, rhubarb, and sage, where they'll get at least six hours of direct sun a day. Part-shade lovers, such as parsley, mint, sorrel, and chives, do well with protection from the harsh, afternoon sun.

Keep pots well watered during the growing season but just moist in the winter and not overwatered. Fertilize with a time-release or organic fertilizer from spring through summer. Some container perennials need regular fertilizer (i.e., chives and parsley), while other herbs (i.e., thyme and rosemary) grow and taste better with less feeding. In cold winter areas, move perennial containers indoors into a cool basement, unheated garage, or shed where the temperatures stay ideally between 32°F and 40°F (0°C and 4°C). Some perennial herbs can be placed on a sunny windowsill in the house to keep them growing, slowly, all winter. For large perennial vegetables that need a dormant period in winter, such as rhubarb and artichoke, a dark, cool basement would be best for their needs.

In spring, repot any vegetables and herbs that are outgrowing their pot or that haven't been repotted for a few years, using new potting soil. Either select one pot size larger or divide or root prune the plants to keep them small. Select offshoots or seedlings to pot up and replace too-large perennials.

Now that you have a good sense of some of the perennial vegetables and herbs you can grow in your continuous vegetable garden, let's take a look at another way to have vegetables perennialize in your garden: by growing vegetables, herbs, and edible flowers that self-sow each year.

Make an edible thriller, filler and spiller container with this rosemary, eggplant, and lemon thyme.

CHAPTER 4

SELF-SOWING VEGETABLES, HERBS, AND EDIBLE FLOWERS

Growing perennial vegetables and herbs is a great way to minimize your work in the garden and maximize your production of delicious edibles. To expand the number of vegetables and herbs you can grow without having to work so hard—and spend as much money—try letting some of those vegetables and herbs self-sow.

Self-sowing vegetables, herbs, and edible flowers were a revelation to me many years ago. I've had a call-in gardening radio show in Vermont for almost thirty years. Early in the show's run, I remember an older caller telling me his special way to plant lettuce. He said in late winter he simply sprinkled the seeds on the snow on his garden beds where he wanted them to grow. He swore it worked every year, and he got earlier crops of lettuce this way with less work. Being a young skeptic, I discounted his advice until I tried it one winter. Low and behold, he was right. The lettuce seeds germinated well before I thought of seeding them or planting transplants outdoors. Then I thought, if this works for sowing lettuce in winter, what about just leaving the bolted lettuce plants to self-sow in fall? And so, my journey into self-sowing as a way to reduce work, and seed costs, and have more fun in the garden began.

Spread bolting lettuce seed heads around the garden to areas where you want lettuce plants next year.

Nasturtiums self-sow readily, but the color of the flower may not be the same as the parent plant.

Like lettuce, mustard self-sows seed readily. The yellow flowers are favorites of pollinators.

WHAT ARE SELF-SOWING VEGETABLES, HERBS, AND EDIBLE FLOWERS?

Self-sowing vegetables, herbs, and edible flowers fall into three categories: annual self-sowers, biennial self-sowers, and perennials that set seed.

Annual self-sowers set and drop seed in summer to germinate and grow a fall crop. Arugula, cilantro, and mustard are good examples of easy-to-grow annual self-sowers. Another way annual self-sowers spread is they set seed in late summer or fall and drop the seed in the garden. These annual self-sowers, such as lettuce, calendula, and leaf fennel, have seed that can overwinter on the ground, even in cold climates, and germinate in spring when the conditions are just right.

Biennial self-sowing vegetables, such as carrots, beets, kale, parsley, and parsnips, grow just leaves and roots the first year in the garden. In warmer climates, or in protected colder gardens, the plants can survive the winter. The second year they put on more vegetative growth, but by early summer they start to flower. After flowering and setting seeds, the plant dies. I often harvest from my Russian kale varieties in spring as they put on new growth. I even harvest the flower stalks to eat, too.

The final group is perennials that self-sow readily. These include nasturtiums, chives, tomatoes, peppers, and violas. Some perennials, such as violas and chives, are cold-tolerant perennials that spread by seeding. Other perennials, such as tomatoes, peppers, nasturtiums, and eggplant, are perennials in warm, tropical climates, but act like annual self-sowers in a colder location. Fruiting plants, such as tomatoes, often have mature fruits that drop to the ground and invariably don't get cleaned up in fall. The seeds overwinter and, in spring, small seedlings of these perennials pop up around where they grew last year. I talk about the "surprise" fruiting plants that often emerge as seedlings in the compost bin from fruits that were collected from the garden in the sidebar on page 85.

Protect young self-sown lettuce seedlings in spring with a row cover if cold weather is in the forecast.

THE ADVANTAGES OF LETTING PLANTS SELF-SOW

Most gardeners are taught to remove plants when they start going to seed in the vegetable garden because it's a signal those plants have "gone by" and are no longer tasty or productive (unless, of course, you *want* to collect and save the seeds for planting next season—more on this practice in chapter 5). It could be that edible greens (lettuce, arugula, cilantro, spinach, etc.) or root crops (radish, beets, turnips, etc.) have bolted and set seed, or that pods or fruits have matured to a stage where they are no longer good to eat (peas, beans, etc.). But in a perpetual vegetable garden, always leave some of these "gone by" plants to mature so they'll self-sow and return to the garden without any help from the gardener.

MOTHER NATURE'S TIMING

One of the key reasons for leaving self-sowing vegetables in the garden is the seed's innate knowledge of optimum germination timing. One of the hardest things for a gardener to keep track of is when to sow the seeds of various vegetables. Is the soil warm enough or too warm to support germination? Does it have too much or too little moisture? Has it been sunny enough? Has the danger of frost really passed? Even with regional charts, tables, and ample online resources, all these questions leave us guessing as to the best time to plant each different vegetable in our garden. But when we let plants self-sow in summer and fall, some of those seeds germinate later that summer and others overwinter in the soil to germinate in the spring, almost always at the best time to support their growth.

Take lettuce, for example. In spring, these seeds know exactly when the best time to germinate is. Not only do we get early crops of lettuce from these savant lettuce seeds, they also tell us when it's time to plant other cool-season crop seeds and transplants. Although there's always a chance of a late frost or freeze, more often than not, these self-sowers have spot-on timing.

Flowering mustard plants are favorites of bees and pollinators.

Self-sown lettuces usually stay true to type, but some may cross, giving you some nice color combinations.

LESS WORK, MORE FREE PLANTS

Another reason for letting some plants self-sow is a reduction in time and money spent. Spring-planted, fast-maturing plants, such as arugula and cilantro, will self-sow and yield one or two new crops in the same year without you having to do anything. It's succession planting without the gardener doing any of the work!

Also, instead of purchasing seeds, preparing beds, and sowing new seeds each year, you can focus on being a garden editor. When a vegetable plant flowers and sets seed, you can cut the mature seedhead off and move it to the bed where you want that plant to grow next year. As the self-sown plants start popping up, decide where they should be growing; you can either leave the self-sown plants where they are or move them to another spot. I often leave robust lettuces in the mulched paths between my beds—as long as they're out of the way—to mature into full edible heads. You can edit out seedlings you don't want growing in the wrong place, and you can transplant the healthiest ones into the beds where you *do* want them to grow.

Of course, you can also collect and save seeds for next year's garden, too. As mentioned, I'll go into more detail on saving seeds in chapter 5. By saving seeds from the healthiest plants, you'll slowly create varieties that are better adapted to your soil, climate, and garden environment.

Another fun part of self-sowing is that sometimes you get crosses happening that yield unusual varieties. I've seen seedlings from self-sown lettuces have unusual leaf color variations. I get some unusual color variations on nasturtium and calendula flowers as well.

SELF-SOWN DISEASE POTENTIAL

Diseases can also be a concern with self-sown vegetables. Tomatoes and potatoes that grow out of a compost pile in spring or self-sow in the garden can harbor harmful diseases, such as late blight, which can wreak havoc in your garden. This is where you'll need to be diligent about watching for signs of these diseases if you're attempting to grow self-sown tomato seedlings or new potato plants from overwintered tubers. I discuss more about saving tubers and bulbs such as potatoes, garlic, and sweet potatoes in chapter 5.

Here are some fall baby mustards that sprouted from a mother plant that dropped seed in summer.

CONCERNS WITH SELF-SOWING

It's not all sunshine and roses with self-sowing seedlings, though. There are some concerns that you should remember. I mentioned how I often get so many self-sown lettuces and mustards that I have plenty to move around the garden. Well, that also means I get *too many* and have to do some weeding, as well as transplanting, especially when they self-sow in the "wrong" places. You can direct this somewhat by placing seed heads in areas where you want seedlings next spring or by saving seeds. Some plants also can self-sow so thickly you have to thin them out to get productive plants.

Another concern is variety crossing. Although many plants, such as lettuce and beans, are naturally self-pollinating and saved or dropped seeds grow to look just like the mother plant, other plants are not self-pollinating and there can be variations in color, size, form, and flavor in the next generation. I like the surprise of what gets created through natural crossing, but other gardeners may be disappointed with the results. Certainly, vegetables that are pollinated by insects and readily cross-pollinate, such as squashes, cucumbers, melons, and pumpkins, will form all types of odd fruits on the plants grown from self-sown seeds. Just look at your compost pile "volunteers" in summer to see what the results might be.

The same goes for the self-sown offspring of hybrid varieties—you never know what you're going to get. You will not get the same color flowers nor the same plant characteristics as the original hybrids, so I usually stick with only letting open-pollinated and heirloom varieties self-sow. But, unless you control the crossing by pollinating the flowers yourself, even open-pollinated versions can be unique. I talk more about this phenomenon in the sidebar on Compost Pile Surprise on page 85.

The growth rate and production of self-sown plants can be affected as well. Sometimes self-sown seedlings won't be as vigorous as freshly seeded versions.

TECHNIQUES FOR GROWING SELF-SOWN PLANTS

Some of the concerns discussed in the previous section can be alleviated by using certain gardening techniques. A lot will depend on the type of gardener you are and your mood for that year. One year, I just decided to let nature take its course and let self-sowing lettuces, arugula, mustards, calendula, nasturtiums, and other plants pop up wherever they wanted. It was chaos with seedlings growing in pathways, under perennial plants, and often overcrowding themselves. As a result, none really grew well. Lesson learned. I'm back to being more restrained.

Now, I'm less likely to let self-sowing just happen randomly in the garden. A good example is my lettuce plants. I often let a few different varieties of lettuce plants bolt and set seed. Instead of just letting the seeds drop where they may, I cut the seed head off once the flowers pass and seeds start to set, and I move the cut seed head to another bed. Often I will either just drop the seed head there, or, if the seeds are already starting to drop off the head, I sprinkle the seeds around where I'd like them next year. This part of editing makes for less work next year in terms of weeding and thinning out random seedlings where I don't want them. For flowers, such as calendula, I also try to deadhead some of the spent flowers to prevent the excessive self-sowing.

Another way of directing where the seedlings grow is to remove the seed head before it starts dropping seeds and save seeds indoors for sowing next year (see chapter 5). This traditional way of sowing seeds really puts you in charge of what grows where.

White, fluffy lettuce flowers and seeds are held tightly together until the seed matures and drops.

FAVORITE SELF-SOWING VEGETABLES, HERBS, AND EDIBLE FLOWERS

There are many self-sowing vegetables, herbs, and edible flowers. Here are some of my favorites to grow in our perpetual garden. I mention if each plant is an annual (in most climates), biennial, or perennial, and other aspects that are important to know about how they self-sow. I purposely don't go into the details of growing each plant since that information is easily obtained in other books and online.

ARUGULA (ANNUAL)

Arugula (*Eruca sativa*) grows best in the cool conditions of spring and fall. The plants become spicy tasting quickly with heat, water, or other stresses, and will bolt. Since arugula grows quickly in spring, plant it where you'd like more seedlings in fall so when it self-sows, you don't have to move seedlings around as much. Arugula seeds will overwinter in the garden. Protect overwintering seeds in cold climates with mulch or a hoop tunnel covered in plastic (see page 166).

Arugula produces lots of seeds, so it can become weedy. It will need to be thinned during good seed-setting years. If you don't thin the seedlings, the plants will be stressed and bolt more quickly.

BORAGE (ANNUAL)

Borage (*Borago officinalis*) grows quickly from seed into a 1 to 2-foot (30 to 61 cm)-tall-and-wide plant with attractive, star-shaped, blue flowers that bees love. Borage self-sows readily, and the seed overwinters in the soil well. I often have borage popping up in pathways and other beds.

I don't use borage for medicinal or other purposes, so I mostly grow it for the pollinators and for its beauty. I often weed out all but three or four plants that have self-sown in suitable locations in the garden, so each plant doesn't take up valuable space.

BEET, CARROT, AND SWISS CHARD (BIENNIAL)

Beet (*Beta vulgaris*) and Swiss chard (*Beta vulgaris* subsp. *cicla*) varieties can easily cross-pollinate with other beet and Swiss chard varieties. Carrots can cross with other carrot varieties and wild carrots. This will create self-sown varieties that may not have the same look and taste as the original plants.

These plants are biennial and won't form seed heads until their second year. You'll need to leave some beet and carrot roots and Swiss chard plants in the garden the first year to overwinter. They will need protection from temperatures

Borage self-sows readily in our garden and we keep a few plants each year for the pollinators.

below 20°F (-7°C) to survive. I've found beet roots and Swiss chard plants are less hardy than carrot roots. Flower stalks and seed heads will form early the second summer. Seeds will drop and overwinter to produce new plants the third year.

While allowing beet, carrot, and Swiss chard plants to self-sow does reduce work in the garden, it ties up that bed area with these plants for three years. This may be problematic if you're trying to rotate different vegetables in the beds. Instead of letting them self-sow in the same bed, you could harvest the seed the second year to sow in another bed the third year. Also, wherever they grow, self-sown carrots, beets, and Swiss chard still need thinning to produce good-sized roots and plants.

CALENDULA (ANNUAL)

Calendula (*Calendula officinalis*) is a low-growing annual with yellow to orange-colored flowers that are edible. I planted calendula once, many years ago, and have self-sowing seedlings each spring that flower in summer. I haven't planted new seed since then.

Calendula is a rampant self-sower, producing many seedlings in spring and summer. Self-sown plants may have variations in the flower colors, but they usually stay in the yellow to orange color range.

Because calendula self-sows so readily and the seed can last more than one year in the soil and still germinate, you may have to weed out 95 percent of the calendula seedlings each spring. You'll also have to keep up with the ongoing germination of seedlings in summer or the plants will get overcrowded, not flower well, and become less attractive.

Calendula flowers self-sow so well, you'll need to thin some out each spring.

CHAMOMILE (ANNUAL OR PERENNIAL)

Roman chamomile (*Chamaemelum nobile*) is a perennial while German chamomile (*Matricaria recutita*) is a self-sowing annual. Both plants have similar growth characteristics, such as small, white, daisylike flowers, ferny foliage, and the same sweet scent and relaxing qualities for use in teas and baths. Roman chamomile grows short while German chamomile can reach a few feet (about 1 m) tall.

Roman chamomile spreads by underground roots, so this section will focus on the self-sowing German chamomile. German chamomile is like calendula in that it self-sows readily, and seedlings will germinate from spring into summer.

Because of the rampant self-sowing, it's best to remove most of the German chamomile seedlings in spring, spacing the remaining plants 3 inches (8 cm) apart for the best flower production. Continue weeding out seedlings in summer.

Cucamelon fruits are cute. These tiny fruits look like a watermelon but taste like a lemony cucumber.

CILANTRO (ANNUAL)

Cilantro (*Coriandrum sativum)* is a popular herb that produces the best leaves with cool weather and moist soils. As soon as it gets hot or stressed, the plant bolts, forming flowers and then seeds. It's best grown in early spring and fall in most climates.

Cilantro creates lots of seeds (which are also known as coriander). Usually, the seeds drop to the soil in summer and germinate when the weather cools, if there is enough moisture. It's easy to get two crops in one year by letting your cilantro self-sow.

Cilantro can drop many seeds, and they will need to be thinned to prevent overcrowding. Overcrowded seedlings is one of the reasons for early bolting and low leaf production. Cilantro seed will also overwinter in most gardens to germinate the following spring, but again, it will need thinning.

CUCAMELON (ANNUAL)

Cucamelons (*Melothria scabra)* have cucumber-like vines that produce small fruits resembling tiny watermelons. The flavor is slightly sour with a crunchy texture.

In tropical climates, cucamelon can be a perennial, growing from underground tubers each year. Most gardeners treat them as annuals, though. The seeds often overwinter from fruits invariably left behind. In spring, new plants emerge when the temperature and moisture conditions are right. Cucamelons usually don't cross with other members of the cucumber family.

Because cucamelons are so prolific, there may be many seedlings in spring that will need to be weeded out. Space plants of the remaining seedlings 1 foot (30 cm) apart.

DILL (ANNUAL)

Dill (*Anethum graveolens*) is an herb that can be eaten three ways. The ferny greens, yellow flowers, and seeds are all edible and are used in a variety of recipes. Dill grows best in spring or fall when the weather is cool and soil moist. Its summer flowers are a boon to pollinators.

Dill can self-sow in late summer and drop seed that either will germinate and grow ferns before a frost or overwinter and grow new plants in spring.

Dill is another herb I planted once and haven't planted again. It always self-sows in our garden, and the seedlings emerge in early spring. Dill isn't easy to transplant unless you dig it when the seedlings are only 3 to 4 inches (8 to 10 cm) tall. It's best to cut seed heads and sprinkle the seed in the areas you want it to grow next year.

FENNEL (MOSTLY ANNUAL, BUT SOMETIMES A BIENNIAL AND PERENNIAL)

Fennel (*Foeniculum vulgare*) is a vegetable and herb related to dill. Bulb fennel is less hardy than leaf fennel, but both have the same anise flavor. In warm climates or in warm winters in cold climates, fennel can be a short-lived perennial. I have plants that are three years old in our New England garden.

Fennel can self-sow readily if allowed to flower and set seed. When harvesting bulb fennel, you destroy the plant. But grow extra plants to allow them to flower for pollinators. In spring, I often find fennel seedlings popping up around the garden. Leaf fennel is a biennial and usually flowers and sets seed the second year.

Like dill, fennel can set lots of seed and doesn't transplant easily. Cut seed heads once the seeds set and move them to parts of the garden where you want fennel to grow next year. Also, thin fennel seedlings in spring to 1 foot (30 cm) apart.

We plant extra fennel each year and let some go to flower. The flowers attract all types of beneficial insects.

LETTUCE (ANNUAL)

Loose leaf lettuce (*Lactuca sativa*) varieties, such as 'Oakleaf', are best to let self-sow. Loose leaf lettuce will form an edible, small head in as little as one month, but you can start harvesting lettuce leaves as soon as enough of them have formed. Lettuce grows best in the cool conditions of spring and fall, but there are some varieties, such as 'Heatwave', that can withstand the summer heat.

Lettuce grows quickly and stays in the leaf stage as long as heat, moisture, or weather stresses don't occur. If stressed, the plant quickly bolts. But that is an advantage because the plants self-sow readily, dropping seeds that will germinate.

Thin self-sown seedlings to 6 to 8 inches (15 to 20 cm) apart or harvest them young. Take seed heads and drop them or sprinkle the seeds in new areas in summer or fall for next year's crop.

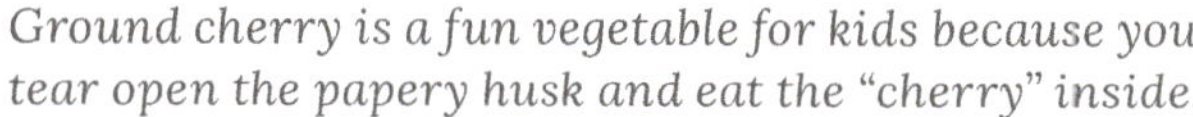

Ground cherry is a fun vegetable for kids because you tear open the papery husk and eat the "cherry" inside.

Kale is a biennial. In our garden, it overwinters and flowers in spring. We eat the spring leaves, then let it flower and set seeds.

GROUND CHERRY (ANNUAL)

Ground cherry (*Physalis peruviana*) is a low-growing tomato relative that forms a fruit in a papery husk in summer. The yellow-colored "cherry" fruit inside the husk is sweet and delicious. Ground cherries grow in the same conditions as tomatoes.

Ground cherry fruits are loaded with small seeds. If you miss some fruits when harvesting, you'll get new seedlings sprouting up the following spring. Ground cherry is another vegetable that I don't have to plant each spring as there are many seedlings popping up in the garden.

Seeds easily overwinter in our garden. In spring, ground cherry seedlings are easy to transplant to new locations. You could move the fruits in fall to where you want them to sprout next spring, but honestly, transplanting them in spring is just as easy. Ground cherries can self-sow liberally, so thin out plants and space transplants or thinned plants 18 to 24 inches (46 to 61 cm) apart.

KALE (BIENNIAL)

Kale (*Brassica oleracea* var. *sabellica*) is a cool-weather–loving vegetable that can overwinter, even in temperatures as low as -10°F (-23°C), and especially with some protection. In spring of the next year, it will regrow and eventually form a flower and set seed. It's best to harvest leaves before the flower's set seed for the best texture and flavor.

If kale plants survive the winter, they will flower and set seed in early summer. The seed will drop, germinate, and potentially yield a fall crop of young greens. Thin kale seedlings in summer or fall, after self-sowing, to 1 foot (30 cm) apart for best growth.

Parsley is a biennial that flowers and sets seed in the spring of its second year.

MUSTARD (MOSTLY ANNUAL)

Annual mustards (*Brassica juncea*), such as 'Green Wave' and 'Red Giant', grow quickly in the cool weather of spring or fall. They can be harvested whenever a sufficient number of leaves have formed. Mustards will bolt with heat or water stress.

Like lettuce, mustard self-sows readily and, if you have a long enough growing season, the seeds can germinate in late summer to form edible young plants in fall. Otherwise, seeds overwinter to germinate the following spring.

Mustard seedlings need thinning in fall or spring to 12 inches (30 cm) apart. Weed out extra seedlings. Move seedlings in late summer to areas of the garden where you want mustard greens next year. Protect seedings in cold climates.

NASTURTIUM (MOSTLY ANNUALS)

Nasturtium (*Tropaeolum majus*) varieties are either mounding or climbing types. They're succulent plants with yellow, orange, or red flowers. The leaves and flowers are edible with a spicy taste. Nasturtiums can be a perennial (and weedy) in frost-free areas.

Nasturtiums set seed readily in late summer or fall depending on the location. Seeds overwinter and new plants grow in spring. Nasturtiums bloom prolifically all summer and can set lots of seeds. Thinning the seedlings is important in spring to space plants 1 to 2 feet (30 to 61 cm) apart. Flower colors in self-sown nasturtiums may vary from the mother plants.

PARSLEY (BIENNIAL)

Parsley (*Petroselinum crispum*) grows best in cool conditions but is a strong grower all season long in my garden. This tap-rooted herb doesn't like to be transplanted. It can tolerate frosts and is a good plant to bring indoors in winter for cooking. See more on bringing plants indoors in chapter 9.

If parsley survives the winter, it will send up a seed stalk in late spring. I often harvest leaves from my overwintered parsley until the flower stalk forms. Then the leaf texture gets tough and the taste less appealing. Seeds that form and drop will overwinter and grow the following spring.

Radish seed pods form quickly after the radish bolts. The pods are edible.

Like other biennials, self-sowing parsley plants will stay in the same bed for three years if the self-sown seeds are allowed to germinate in year three. You can also collect seed in the fall of year two to sow elsewhere. Move self-sown seedlings when they're very young to avoid stunting the plant.

RADISH (ANNUAL OR BIENNIAL)

Most radishes (*Raphanus sativus*) are annuals that grow quickly in the cool spring to form a red- or white-skinned root. They will bolt with warm weather, forming flowers and eventually seed heads. Winter radish varieties take longer to form a root and are mostly biennials, forming a flower and seed stalk the next spring.

Radish roots and seed heads are edible. Some people collect the seed pods for eating as well as resowing. Radishes will drop seed in summer and, if the growing season is long enough, some seed will grow in fall and form small roots. Otherwise, the seed overwinters to germinate in spring.

Radishes can set a lot of seed, so seedlings need to be thinned to about 4 inches (10 cm) apart to get edible roots. You can allow radishes to drop seed in late summer in the same bed or harvest the seed heads and move them to a new bed for spring growing.

SPINACH (ANNUAL OR BIENNIAL)

In most areas, spinach (*Spinacia oleracea*) is either an annual or biennial. In cold climate areas, spinach will grow well in cool conditions and bolt once it gets warm. In warmer areas, spinach can be fall planted and will bolt the following spring. It's best to grow spinach in the cool conditions of spring or fall for the best flavor and texture of the leaves.

Like all cool-loving greens, spinach will bolt when confronted with heat, drought, or stressful conditions. Spinach flower heads form, dropping seed. In my garden, the seed usually doesn't germinate until the following spring. In warm areas you may see spinach seeds germinating in fall of the same year.

Spinach seedlings can be finicky about transplanting. Sow seeds collected from seed heads in areas where you want spinach the following year.

Sunflowers form hundreds of seeds. Those the birds, mice, and chipmunks don't get will germinate the following spring in your garden.

SUNFLOWER (ANNUAL)

I grow sunflowers (*Helianthus annuus*) for the edible seeds and also for the birds. Birds are good cleaners of sunflower heads. The best varieties for self-sowing are the heirloom and open-pollinated varieties and those with large seeds. Avoid specialty, sterile seed varieties such as 'Teddy Bear'.

Sunflowers readily self-sow in my garden, even after the birds seem to have cleaned them all out, popping up in a variety of locations the following spring. They transplant easily if you dig them when they're small.

If birds don't eat too many of your sunflower seeds, you'll have an abundance of seedlings in spring that will need to be thinned, moved, or discarded. You can also harvest the emerging sprouts and add them to salads.

CHERRY TOMATO (MOSTLY ANNUAL)

Tomatoes (*Solanum lycopersicum*) are tropical perennial plants mostly treated as annuals. You can overwinter individual plants, however, even in a cold climate. See chapter 5 for instructions for overwintering tomato plants.

As most gardeners already know from the tomato seedlings that pop up in the garden each spring, tomatoes do self-sow readily. For the quickest maturing self-sown tomatoes, choose heirloom or open-pollinated varieties, such as 'Black Cherry' and 'Matt's Wild Cherry' to self-sow. Hybrid varieties that self-sow will not come back with the same traits of the parents. Self-sown larger-fruited tomato varieties will take longer to mature. It's best to collect larger-fruited varieties and save the seeds for spring planting as described in chapter 5.

Allow some of the cherry tomato fruits to drop to the ground to self-sow. Tomato seeds will overwinter in the soil and germinate when conditions are right the following spring. Select the strongest and healthiest of the volunteer seedlings when small and move them to their new bed.

Caution! Self-sown tomatoes can harbor diseases that can affect your whole tomato crop and even other tomato family plants. Be careful to weed out all tomato seedlings you are not saving to grow and be watchful for any diseases that develop on those saved volunteer plants.

You can grow self-sown tomatoes but watch out for diseases on the fruits and plants.

Dandelion greens are tasty and cultivated varieties can be eaten all summer.

Lamb's-quarters' greens are best eaten when the leaves are young.

WILD EDIBLES THAT SELF-SOW

There's another group of self-sowing edibles that I've really come to embrace over the years. Self-sowing wild greens provide easy-to-harvest, delicious greens for salads and cooking. These nutrient dense greens are loaded with vitamins and minerals.

For me it all goes back to my Italian grandparents' farm. As a little boy, I remember watching my Italian relatives from New York City come up to the farm for the weekend in spring and go into the fields to collect dandelion greens. They would come back with baskets filled with the greens, which my grandmother would cook with garlic, olive oil, and tomatoes to make a delicious lunch with homemade bread.

I still collect wild dandelion greens in spring, and I grow some nice cultivated varieties, too. I also gather lamb's-quarters, wild amaranth, purslane, and chickweed. In the continuous vegetable garden, it's fun to let some of these wild greens self-sow for quick and easy meals. Here are some of my favorite wild greens.

Note: Check local resources to identify wild greens in your region and always remember to properly identify them before harvesting. Also, harvest plants growing in places away from roads, pesticide spraying, and pollutants, and always taste test a few of the greens first to see how your body reacts to them.

DANDELION (*TARAXACUM OFFICINALE*)

Everyone knows common dandelions mostly for their beautiful yellow flowers in spring and summer. Considered a lawn weed by most people, common dandelions also have delicious, tender young greens in spring. The leaves turn bitter once the plant flowers. If you're really into dandelions, the flowers and roots are also edible.

Common dandelions are short-lived perennials. This Eurasian edible flower is a good source of pollen for bees. While collecting greens from the common dandelion is easy, I'd suggest growing the cultivated versions from the chicory family. The Italian dandelion (*Cichorium intybus*) is probably the one my Italian relatives were remembering when they saw the common dandelions in Connecticut. The leaves look very similar, and the flavor has the same combination of sweetness and bitterness. Unlike wild dandelions, varieties such as 'Felix', 'Clio', and 'Italiko Red' are slow to go to seed and can be recut repeatedly in summer, producing an abundance of greens all season long. Certainly the young greens are the most tender, but the older greens still are tasty when cooked.

Amaranth greens are tasty and highly nutritious.

SELF-SOWING

Common dandelions self-sow abundantly from seeds attached to the iconic, white, puffball seed heads. Just look at your lawn in spring! They will spread throughout your garden and landscape, requiring only a bit of open soil to germinate.

The Italian version is a short-loved perennial. The first year it produces mostly greens. In subsequent years, a classic, sky-blue flower emerges. You'll recognize the wild version of this Italian dandelion as our roadside chicory weed in summer. Harvest the leaves while young for the best flavor.

The Italian dandelion also self-sows, but the seeds are larger and heavier, so they tend to stay close to the mother plant unless moved by humans or animals. Dandelions prefer loose, well-drained soil and full sun. Once established, dandelions will be a fixture in your garden until you don't want them anymore.

LAMB'S-QUARTERS (*CHENOPODIUM GIGANTIUM*)

Lamb's-quarters is so named for an ancient English harvest festival. This is a common annual weed in many cultivated gardens, but it's actually a great wild green. It's in the goosefoot plant family, related to quinoa (*Chenopodium album*). In fact, lamb's-quarters can produce quinoa grain seeds, but not as well or in the same abundance as the true quinoa plant, and the seed heads take a long time to mature.

It's the greens that are easiest for the continuous vegetable gardener to cultivate. While common lamb's-quarters varieties are green, there are more colorful selections. 'Magenta Spreen' has bright pink coloring on younger leaves, making it a colorful and tasty addition to salads. The flavor is similar to spinach. The nutritious spring leaves are best for fresh eating, but you can harvest and cook young leaves anytime from older plants throughout the growing season.

SELF-SOWING

Lamb's-quarters self-sows readily, in response to heat and long days, spreading thousands of seeds in summer. Once you have a mature plant in your garden, you'll probably have seedlings forever. This cool-season edible likes moist, fertile soil and sun to grow. Thin out young, emerging plants in spring for use in salads or as microgreens. Thinning also gives the remaining plants more room to grow.

Mature plants drop seed that will overwinter to grow as next year's crop. You'll only need to save a few mature plants for self-sowing. You can also skip years because lamb's-quarters seeds can last for years in the soil, and they all don't germinate at once. Lightly cultivate the soil in spring to bring them to the surface to germinate.

AMARANTH (*AMARANTHUS RETROFLEXUS*)

A common name of this species of amaranth is red-rooted pigweed. That doesn't sound very appealing, but amaranth is a great spring green. It's a popular staple in other countries, such as Jamaica, where it's known as callaloo. Like lamb's-quarters, the green leaves are nutritious and mild tasting, especially when picked young. Red-rooted pigweed is easy to identify from the red roots and oval leaf shape with serrated edges.

Purslane sprouts during warm weather producing crisp, slightly sour leaves and stems.

Chickweed is a summer grower that makes a great addition to pesto.

Amaranth grows best in full sun on warm, compost-amended, well-drained soils. It tolerates poor fertility, compacted soils, and can reach 2 to 4 feet (61 to 122 cm) tall in late summer. Like lamb's-quarters, the young leaves are best for eating raw or cooked.

SELF-SOWING

Amaranth plants are annuals that can produce 100,000 seeds in one season. Having seedlings to harvest isn't a problem. Having too many, may be. It's best to harvest in spring and let only a few plants mature for next year's crop. The seeds can overwinter for a number of years, so you could probably skip a year or two and still have seedlings in spring.

PURSLANE (*PORTULACA OLERACEA*)

Common purslane is an annual weed in many flower and vegetable gardens. Purslane is becoming increasingly popular for its mild, sour-tasting, crisp, succulent leaves and stems in salads, soups, stews, and sauces. There are even varieties of purslane, such as 'Goldberg Golden', that feature orange stems and greenish-yellow leaves. It has larger leaves than the wild purslane version.

Like all portulacas, purslane loves to grow in full sun in well-drained soil. The seeds need sunlight to germinate. I often see purslane growing in our raised beds in summer after the soil has warmed. Purslane stems will root at the nodes. It can form a 2-foot (61 cm)-diameter mat, if grown well. Harvest the leaves and stems for salads. Harvesting also stimulates more growth. Purslane is very frost sensitive.

SELF-SOWING

Purslane produces tiny seeds in abundance. Once you have the plant in your garden and it sows seeds, you'll have purslane forever. The small seeds are released by the seed pods and can stay in the soil for decades. Purslane should be monitored in spring and summer, and excessive plants should be removed. Like lamb's-quarters and amaranth, extra plants are good as chicken feed.

CHICKWEED (*STELLARIA MEDIA*)

Chickweed is a late spring, annual weed that grows quickly in warm soils and full sun. The plants have small leaves, which can be harvested for use in salads and cooked like spinach. I've used chickweed to make pesto.

There are a number of species of chickweed. Most of them form a mat of green foliage in areas with bare ground. They won't compete well with established plantings or in meadows. Chickweed plants like moisture and often are found on stream banks and wet areas. Pollinators enjoy the flowers while birds and wildlife feed on the seeds and foliage. Chickweed got its name from being a favorite food of chickens.

SELF-SOWING

Chickweed sets thousands of seeds per plant each year, and once established will be in your yard for years. It is shallow rooted, so extra plants are removed easily. Look for this wild edible in summer when it starts to really grow with the warm weather. Since it doesn't compete well with established plantings, keeping the soil planted or mulched is an effective way to slow its spread.

If you have a garden personality that wants more control in the garden and is a little uncomfortable with all this self-sowing, then the next chapter is for you. I'll discuss the basics of seed and plant saving with some interesting twists.

COMPOST PILE SURPRISE

Inevitably each spring, I get questions on my radio show about transplanting seedlings that have magically sprouted in a compost pile. They usually are seedlings of squashes and pumpkins that overwinter in rotting fruits and pop up with the warm weather. I've highlighted many self-sowing veggies that are easy to grow in the garden in this part of the book, but some just won't be true to their parents.

Cucurbit family vegetables, such as squash, melons, pumpkins, and zucchini, almost always are cross-pollinated by bees with pollen from different varieties. While the fruits that form will be what you expected, the seeds inside have a different genetic mix. If left in the garden or composted, the next spring the seeds will grow. You'll get some odd-looking pumpkin, melon, or squashlike creatures. I wouldn't depend on them to give you the squashes, melons, or pumpkins you want for home use. They may or may not be tasty and useful.

Cucurbits that sprout in your compost pile and fruit won't be the same as the original plants you grew last year.

If you really want to save seeds of cucurbit family veggies, you'll need to hand-pollinate the flowers of heirloom or open-pollinated varieties yourself. In the morning when the flowers first open, transfer pollen between male and female flowers with a cotton swab or small paintbrush. Then seal the flower so no bees can get in and add more pollen. Let the fruit fully mature, then harvest and dry the seeds and save them indoors over the winter to plant in the spring. Personally, I would rather spend the money on buying fresh seed each year than putting in so much effort!

CHAPTER 5

SEED AND PLANT SAVING

Self-sowing vegetables, herbs, and edible flowers sure can make life easier in the continuous vegetable garden. But sometimes it's best just to collect and save the seeds yourself for planting in spring. The advantage of seed saving is you can harvest seed, clean it well, and store it properly so you get a better germination rate. As I've mentioned earlier in this book, I'm not too interested in achieving record yields from my plants; I just want a consistent supply of vegetables all season long. But that being said, seeds that self-sow are subject to the harsh realities of the weather and may not survive. I have noticed that some springs I get more self-sown seedlings of lettuce, dill, arugula, and mustard popping up than other springs. So, to ensure success, collect and save some seeds to store indoors.

Another way to reduce work and costs, and have some fun, in your continuous vegetable garden is to save bulbs and tubers. You can save garlic bulbs, shallot bulbs, sweet potatoes, and sometimes even potatoes, from year to year to replant (see page 92). I've found that I can slowly adapt a variety to better suit our soil and climate by saving the best from each year's harvest and replanting those plants.

Another option is to take cuttings. Stems from herbs, such as basil, can be rooted as cuttings and grown indoors until spring when they can be replanted. This can save you money and give you a jump on the season.

You can even save whole plants of perennials that are normally treated as annuals, such as globe artichokes, peppers, and tomatoes. When saving the whole plant, you have a mature plant that will produce sooner, and you get the exact variety you want to grow next year.

Let's look at seed saving, bulb and tuber saving, and whole plant saving in detail.

SEED SAVING 101

There are whole books written on seed saving that go into great detail. Here, I'm going to focus on the vegetables, herbs, and edible flowers I think are easiest to save and will lead to the most successful results. There's additional information on seed saving found in the resources section.

Seeds from different plants are collected and saved differently, but there are some standard rules to follow when saving seeds.

RULE #1: SELECT THE EASIEST VEGETABLES AND EDIBLE FLOWERS FROM WHICH TO SAVE SEED

Some vegetables are easier to save seeds from than others. In general, select vegetables that are self-pollinating and less likely to cross with other varieties of that vegetable in your garden. These include beans, peas, soybeans, peppers, tomatoes, lettuce, Asian greens, and radishes. Edible flowers, such as marigolds, calendula, and nasturtiums, are also among the easiest seeds to save. Biennial vegetables, such as carrots, beets, and cabbage family vegetables, take two years to set seed and they cross-pollinate easily with others in their family, making the results of seed saving a bit riskier. Squash, melon, pumpkin, and cucumber are normally pollinated by insects and are more difficult to isolate to prevent cross-pollination, making them among the riskiest for reliable seed saving.

RULE #2: SELECT OPEN-POLLINATED OR HEIRLOOM VARIETIES

Select open-pollinated or heirloom varieties to save seed from. These varieties are the most likely to produce seedlings that are similar to the mother plant (true-to-type) next year. Hybrid varieties have been crossed many times to produce the variety you're growing. This means there is a lot of genetic material in that seed. When grown next year, you won't know what mix of plant genetics and characteristics you'll get. But you can be assured it won't be the same as the mother plant.

Save lettuce seed after flowering but before the seed starts dropping on the ground.

RULE #3: PROTECT AGAINST CROSS-POLLINATION

Even if you select an open-pollinated variety, if you're growing other varieties of that same vegetable nearby, there still is a chance of cross-pollination. To ensure you get the same plant characteristics in the new seeds, cover plants with row covers to prevent insects from transferring pollen from other varieties, grow only one variety of that vegetable, and grow varieties further apart.

Beans are easy to save for replanting next year. Just let the pods and beans totally dry out before storing.

RULE #4: SAVE SEED FROM THE HEALTHIEST PLANTS

Select the healthiest plants and fruits without diseases to save seeds from. Seeds can carry viruses, bacteria, and other diseases with them, so saving seed from diseased plants or fruits can spread those pathogens into next year's garden.

RULE #5: HARVEST SEEDS AT THE RIGHT STAGE OF MATURITY

Harvest the fruits or seed pods at their mature stage. This is often weeks after you would normally harvest these fruits or seed pods for eating.

RULE #6: SEPARATE THE SEED, DRY, AND STORE PROPERLY

After harvesting fruits and seed pods, remove the seed properly to dry and store. Seeds need to be completely dry and stored in an airtight container in a cool, dark location, such as a refrigerator, cool closet, or basement, to stay viable for sowing next year. Label the containers for each vegetable and variety.

Store your seeds in clearly-marked plastic bags for easy access in spring.

THE BEST SEEDS TO SAVE AS A BEGINNER

Even when growing open-pollinated varieties, some will need a distance of many feet between varieties so they don't cross-pollinate. If you're okay with rolling the dice on cross-pollination and the resulting plants, don't worry about separating the varieties. Here are some of the easiest vegetables to save seed from for beginners.

BEANS AND PEAS

Bush bean, pole bean, soybean, pea, lima bean, and fava bean are some of the easiest vegetable seeds to save each year. Separate varieties 10 to 20 feet (3 to 6 m) apart to ensure true-to-type seeds. Dedicate certain plants to save seed from and let the pods fully mature on those plants. This may take up to one month after you'd normally harvest these pods for eating. You can also harvest the pods once they mature—but before they're completely dry—and continue drying the pods and seeds indoors. Once dry, the seeds can be heard rattling inside the pod. Remove the seeds and let them further dry in a cool, dry area, out of direct sunlight for two weeks before storing. Legume seeds can last 3 to 4 years in storage.

EDIBLE ANNUAL FLOWERS

Seeds from edible annual flowers, such as calendula, marigold, and nasturtium, can also be easily saved. However, to get plants that come true to seed, you'll have to separate varieties by a great distance. But if you're okay with a surprise mixture of color varieties, go ahead and save some seeds.

For marigolds, let the flowers mature and set seed pods. Harvest marigold seed pods when the flower petals are dry and the base of the seed pod has turned brown. Remove the dried petals. Marigold seeds look like slivers with the dark seeds attached. When the sliver is brown on the seed end, the seed is ripe.

Calendula seed pods are easy to save. Wait until the brown seeds naturally drop from the flower.

Marigold seeds look like matchsticks and are produced in abundance.

Calendula seed is harvested when the flower has matured, and the seed pod is completely brown and dry. Check every few days by taking a brown paper bag, holding the seed pods over the bag, and rubbing the pods to see if the seeds pop out. When dry, the seeds fall out of the pods easily. Cut the dried flowers to harvest the seeds.

Nasturtium seeds are harvested once the flowers are spent and green seed pods form. The pods form in clusters with two to three pea-sized seeds inside. Once the pods dry out and wrinkle, harvest the seeds.

Dry all of these seeds in a cool, dry place on a paper plate or towel for a few days after harvest and then store. These annual flower seeds can remain viable for up to three years.

LETTUCE AND GREENS

Separate varieties 10 to 20 feet (3 to 6 m) apart in your garden if you're saving seed from multiple varieties and want true-to-type seed. After lettuce plants flower, they will form fluffy seed heads. The seed and fluff in lettuce seed heads are tightly bound together until the seed is mature. A simple way to harvest seed is to check the seed heads every few days by shaking them over a paper bag. Once you see some tiny lettuce seeds dropping into the bag, cut the seed heads and remove all the seeds. Lettuce, and greens such as mustard, won't have much chaff, so they are easy to clean and store. Lettuce seed can last in storage for up to six years.

Wait a few weeks after you normally harvest peppers to harvest fruits for storing the seeds.

Rub the sunflower head after the petals have dropped. The seeds pop off when ready to harvest.

PEPPERS

Separate open-pollinated pepper varieties at least 300 feet (91 m) apart if you're trying to get true-to-type seed. You can also hand-pollinate the flowers with an artist's paintbrush and then cover the plant with a row cover after to avoid cross-pollination. Once the fruits form you can remove the cover. Place a tag on those fruits you hand-pollinated once they form.

Let the fruit mature to the final color stage and wait a few more weeks before harvesting it for seed. Cut around the top of the fruit with a knife and carefully twist the stem to remove the core with seeds. Be careful handling hot pepper seeds as they will have capsicum on them and can be irritating. Dry pepper seeds on newspaper or screens for several days in a cool, dark, dry area. When you can snap a seed easily in half, it's dry enough to store. Peppers can last 3 to 4 years in storage.

RADISHES

Radish flowers can readily cross-pollinate with wild radishes and other cultivated varieties. If you're trying to save a particular variety, it will need to be isolated from other radish varieties by 800 feet (244 m). Let the seed heads form and the pods dry on the plant. The pods won't shatter or easily open even when dry. Harvest the seed pods when they're brown and brittle. Lay the seed pods and stalks on a row cover in a protected location to continue drying for a few days. Crush the pods by hand to open them, remove the seeds. Store them in a cool, dry place. Radish seed can remain viable for up to six years.

SUNFLOWERS

Sunflowers are another fun, edible annual flower to save seeds for eating, bird feeding, and planting next year. As with the other vegetables, select open-pollinated varieties to save seed from. It may be difficult to save the exact variety because bees love to spread sunflower pollen for miles. You can cover the flower head with

Let tomato fruits ripen completely indoors or outdoors then harvest the seeds.

Viable tomato seeds will sink to the bottom of a bowl of water while unviable seeds will float.

mosquito netting to prevent cross-pollination. But you'll have to rub two flowers together or move the pollen with an artist's brush to ensure pollination. Repeat pollinating the flowers daily for about one week.

Let the sunflower heads start to die down. When the back of the head turns a yellow-to-brown color or birds show interest in the seeds, it's time to harvest. Cut the stem off just below the head and bring the head into a cool, airy, dry indoor area, ideally on racks or screens, to continue drying for a few weeks. Watch out for birds and animals. I once stored my sunflower heads in our garage and forgot about them for a few days. When I checked, mice had eaten most of the seeds.

When you can rub the flower head and the seeds naturally dislodge, it's time to remove all the seeds. Clean them and store the seed in a sealed container in a cool, dry place.

TOMATOES

Tomato seeds have a few more steps to saving them properly. Separate open-pollinated varieties by at least 10 feet (3 m) to get seeds that will be true-to-type. Harvest the fruits when they're fully mature and ready to eat. The seeds will be mature then as well. You'll only need a few fruits to get plenty of seeds.

Squeeze the pulp from the fruit into a container of water. Allow the container, filled with water, seeds, and pulp, to sit in a warm (80°F [27°C]) room out of sunlight for one to four days to ferment. Fermentation helps the seeds separate from the pulp. Once mold forms on the top, it's time to separate the good and bad seeds. The viable seeds will sink to the bottom of the liquid while the unviable seeds will float on top of the container. Skim off the foam and unviable seeds and discard. Pour the remaining liquid and viable seeds into a strainer and rinse the seeds clean. Remove the seeds and dry for five to seven days on a paper plate, coffee filter, or glass dish in a cool, dry location. Don't use a paper towel as the seeds will stick to it. Tomato seeds can remain viable for five to ten years. Store the seed in a sealed container in a cool, dry place.

SAVING BULBS AND TUBERS

Seeds aren't the only way to save your plants from one year to the next. Vegetables that reproduce from bulbs and tubers are also good candidates. Garlic, shallot, sweet potato, and potato are the most common vegetables to save this way. Not only do you save money not having to purchase the bulbs or tubers in spring or fall to plant, but also over time you can select and replant the healthiest and largest bulbs and tubers. This will slowly create a variety that is more adapted to your soil and climate and more to your liking.

GARLIC AND SHALLOT

We've been growing garlic and shallots for years, and I only bought them once. Garlic and shallot bulbs are planted in fall, overwintered, and then harvested in early summer. As you harvest, save the biggest and best bulbs and then replant them in fall. In doing this, you can select for size and quality. Over time, you'll end up creating varieties adapted to your specific gardening environment by saving the best ones and replanting them each year. Here's how to grow garlic and shallots and save them for planting.

Purchase garlic and shallot bulbs from a reputable source, selecting the types and varieties you like. Hardneck garlic (*Allium sativum* var. *ophioscorodon*) forms seed heads known as scapes that are edible and a spring treat, while softneck garlic (*Allium sativum* var. *sativum*) has supple leaves that are good for braiding. Softneck garlic varieties store the longest of any type of garlic and are best for long-term storage. That being said, for replanting, you only have

Break apart garlic bulbs the night before planting into cloves so they can be ready to plant.

to wait a few months between harvesting and planting, so either type will do. We've saved our hard necks for years and replanted them without any problems. Shallots (*Allium cepa*) come in yellow and red varieties and are planted in much the same way as garlic. They can also be planted in spring for a summer harvest.

For both garlic and shallots, plant the bulbs in the fall, or spring for shallots, three to five weeks before your ground typically freezes. For garlic, the night before planting, break the head apart into cloves and let them sit overnight. This will help the basal plate callus over for better rooting and less chance of disease organisms entering. Plant garlic cloves or shallot bulbs in compost-amended raised beds, 2 inches (5 cm) deep and 6 inches (15 cm) apart, pointy-side up. Cover with hay, straw, or chopped leaves and secure the mulch against winds.

Come spring, with the first signs of new growth, remove the mulch, then water and weed. In early summer, once the bottom garlic leaves turn yellow, carefully dig up the bulbs. With shallots, the bulb will split into multiple bulbs on the soil surface. Once the leaves start to die back and the bulbs split, harvest them.

For both garlic and shallots, save the smallest cloves and bulbs for eating and the largest ones for replanting in fall. We store them in our cool basement under turned-over clay pots to keep them moist for fall planting and winter eating. Our summer-harvested garlic and shallots often last well into the next spring.

For longer storage of garlic bulbs, place them under clay pots in a cool, dark basement and the bulbs can last until next summer.

Store seed potatoes separate from the ones you're eating to prevent disease spread.

Let potatoes cure on racks to toughen their skin for better storage.

POTATO

Gardeners have been saving potato tubers for replanting for thousands of years. There is a legitimate concern, however, about saving diseased tubers that can spread the disease to other members of the *Solanaceae* family. You must be careful to keep your plants healthy and disease-free when growing. Select varieties, such as 'Yukon Gold', that naturally last longer in storage. Remember these seed potatoes will have to last until planting time next spring.

Let plants that you'll be saving seed potatoes from die completely to the ground before harvesting. They'll have thicker skins and last longer in storage. Save only the healthiest and cleanest potatoes for replanting and separate those spuds from the rest of your stored potatoes right after harvest.

To save your seed potatoes, let them cure on racks or screens in a well-ventilated, warm room or shed for two weeks. The curing will toughen the skin and extend the storage time. Gently clean off the soil by hand.

Bring them into a dark room that stays between 35°F and 40°F (2°C and 4°C). Warmer temperatures will force the potatoes to sprout earlier. Store them in well-ventilated containers such as perforated cardboard boxes. Cover with newspaper or cardboard. Don't store potatoes near any fruits or onions because they emit ethylene gas, which causes the spuds to sprout early. Check weekly and remove any spuds that are rotting. Plant in spring even if the potatoes are wrinkled. Cut the spuds so each piece has at least two eyes.

If you see any signs of severe diseases, such as late blight, in storage, you should destroy the entire crop. The same is true when growing out your saved potatoes.

Sweet potato sprouts emerge from eyes on the overwintered tubers. Cut, root, and grow those sprouts for new plants.

SWEET POTATO

Like potatoes, sweet potatoes can be stored and used in spring for making new plants. Unlike potatoes, there is less concern about diseases. Let your sweet potato plants grow until frost kills the foliage, but the cold doesn't affect the tubers. Remove the foliage, harvest, and cure as you would potatoes. Let them dry for twenty-four hours.

Sweet potatoes plants are grown in spring from slips (rooted sprouts) growing from eyes on the tuber. The best tubers for slip making are the smaller tubers. Eat the large ones and save the small ones—about two inches (5 cm) in diameter—for making slips. Keep the sweet potatoes you'll use for growing slips separate from the ones you'll be eating. Store them in a ventilated box in a dark room with temperatures between 50°F and 60°F (10°C and 16°C). Lower temperatures cause the skins to thicken and aren't good for slip making. Higher temperatures cause the tubers to prematurely sprout.

Six to eight weeks before your last frost date, remove the slip sweet potatoes from storage. Place them somewhere in the house where it's light, warm, and humid, such as the kitchen. This will initiate slip formation on the tuber. Keep the tubers sitting sideways to produce the most slips. Some gardeners place the tubers in a shallow tray of water to keep them plump. You can usually produce eight to fifteen slips per tuber.

Once the slips are 2 inches (5 cm) long, gently remove them and compost the tuber. Root the slips in pots filled with moistened, lightweight potting soil placed in a bright room out of the direct sunlight. You can also root slips by just placing them in water to form roots. Once roots form, plant the rooted slips in soil for healthier roots. Grow in pots for four weeks until the slips are well rooted and the weather is warm enough to transplant them into the garden.

TAKING CUTTINGS

Another way to save plants for next year is to take stem cuttings. Some vegetables, and many herbs, can be propagated easily by cuttings. Take and root the cuttings in fall and overwinter the plant for replanting in spring. The main benefits of cuttings are:

1. You get the same variety next year, ready to plant come spring.
2. You overwinter a smaller version of your favorite variety so it takes up less space.
3. You save money not buying new transplants.

Of course, you'll have to be sure the cuttings are disease-free and rooted well so the plant will grow quickly to maturity.

WHAT PLANTS CAN BE CUT?

The easiest vegetables to take cuttings from are tomatoes, tomatillos, and peppers. Many herbs, such as basil, thyme, oregano, rosemary, lavender, sage, and mint, can also be propagated by stem cuttings. Here are some details on taking stem cuttings.

HOW TO TAKE A CUTTING

Take and root stem cuttings in late summer or fall. Select a healthy, upright stem from a healthy plant. This is particularly important for tomatoes since they are often prone to foliar diseases. For tomatoes, you can also cut a sucker.

Cut the stem below a set of leaves about 4 to 6 inches (10 to 15 cm) from the tip of the stem. Remove all but the top set of leaves. Dip the cut end in rooting hormone powder to hasten root growth and stick the cutting in a small pot filled with moistened potting soil. You can also simply place the bottom of the cutting in a cup of water. Once the roots start to form, then transplant it into potting soil. I like using rooting hormone powder in soil because the roots form faster and are stronger than roots forming in water. This is especially true for peppers, lavender, rosemary, and sage.

Taking cuttings is an easy way to overwinter a smaller basil plant and save the same variety as last year.

Place the cuttings to root in a sunny window or under grow lights. See chapter 9 for more on growing plants under grow lights. As the plants grow, you can also snip off additional 4 to 6 inch (10 to 15 cm)-long stem pieces to root. This will make the original cutting bush out more and provide you with plenty of cuttings as the winter continues. Keep the soil evenly moist and the plants away from cold drafts.

In spring, at the right time for your plant, harden off the rooted cuttings and plant them in a container or garden outdoors.

Overwintered globe artichoke plants will send up root sprouts in spring which will become new flowering plants.

SAVING WHOLE PLANTS

Instead of taking just seeds or pieces of your original plant to save and grow again, why not take the whole plant? Many "annual" vegetables are actually perennials in a warm, tropical climate. Some good vegetables to overwinter include tomatoes, peppers, and globe artichokes.

OVERWINTERING GLOBE ARTICHOKE

Globe artichokes are short-lived perennial plants in zones that stay above about 10°F (-12°C) in the winter. They typically produce their edible flower buds in the second year of growth. Many gardeners now grow them as annuals, tricking them into thinking they've gone through a winter by exposing them to cool temperatures in late winter or spring (see page 34). In early spring in warm climates, globe artichoke mother plants also will send out offshoots, or "pups," from the crown. These offshoots can be dug, divided, and replanted. They will form artichoke flowers that year.

If you live in regions with colder winters, the key is to get the artichoke plant through the winter alive. If you live in areas with winter temperatures that go down to about -10°F (-23°C), you can try to mulch the plant heavily in fall as I described in chapter 3.

The second option is to grow your globe artichoke in a 20-inch (51 cm)-diameter plastic container. Protect the container in winter by moving it into an unheated greenhouse, shed, or garage where the temperatures stay above freezing, but below 50°F (10°C). In spring, separate and replant any "pups" that form off the mother plant, and they will flower for you later the same season.

Overwinter mature pepper plants by cutting them back hard and growing them in a cool room in winter.

OVERWINTERING PEPPERS

As anyone living in warmer climates knows, peppers are perennial plants. I've seen pepper plants growing as small bushes that have been alive for years in warmer gardens. Here's how to overwinter your prized pepper plant in a cold location. In late fall: pick off all the peppers; dig up the plant; wash the roots, removing all the soil; and cut the roots back by removing errant roots. Cut back the shoot system so only a few short, *Y*-shaped branches are left coming off the main trunk. While this may seem like you just killed your pepper plant, it will help it survive the winter period.

Repot the pepper and place it in a cool, 50°F to 60°F (10 to 16°C) bright room. Keep the soil barely moist. As the days lengthen, the pepper may start forming leaves. You can let it grow, moving it to a sunnier spot or under grow lights. To slow its growth, place it in a cooler room. By spring, you can repot the plant or transplant it into the garden after hardening it off. The plant will grow faster than new seedling transplants because of the larger root system. It will also produce fruits sooner.

OVERWINTERING TOMATOES

Let's make a Tomato Wrap! The prize for any gardener is having early, ripe tomatoes. If you have a favorite tomato variety you love to grow, here's a way to get that plant to produce earlier each summer. Like peppers, tomatoes are perennials in warmer climates, meaning you can overwinter your tomato indoors in a dormant state. You don't have to grow them under grow lights or hardly fuss with them at all in winter. They'll reward you with earlier and more tomatoes next summer.

1. In fall before a frost, uproot your tomato plant, keeping as much of the root system intact as possible.
2. Cut the stems back to 1 foot (30 cm) tall with no leaves on them. This is also a good way to reduce any diseases from coming in with the plant.
3. Gently remove as much of the soil around the roots as you can with your hand. You can gently wash the roots as well.
4. Cut back long roots and wrap the rest of the roots into a small ball.
5. Lay the tomato and roots on an old T-shirt or piece of cloth. Wrap moistened shredded paper, peat moss, or vermiculite around the roots.
6. Wrap the T-shirt around the wad of moistened and wrapped roots and secure it with string.
7. Wrap plastic wrap or a plastic grocery bag around the T-shirt ball to conserve moisture.
8. Place the tomato ball, with stems sticking out the top, in a cool basement, garage, or even the refrigerator. Keep the temperatures above freezing.
9. Check the root ball every six weeks for moisture and moisten as needed. In late winter, unwrap the tomato, repot it, and let it grow for six weeks before planting in the garden.

The first part of this book has been all about vegetables, herbs, and edible flowers and how to grow them in a more continuous way. Now, I'll move into one of my favorite group of plants: fruits. Let's look at how to incorporate fruiting bushes and trees into your perpetual garden.

You can overwinter your favorite tomato plant by storing it in a dormant state until spring.

CHAPTER 6

A PERPETUAL FRUIT PATCH

When you think of your favorite things to eat from a garden, fruit must come to mind. Who can resist succulent strawberries, blueberries, raspberries, peaches, and other fruits picked fresh from your own plants? But many gardeners shy away from planting fruits for various reasons. Some think they are too hard to grow and take years to produce. Others feel they don't have the space to grow them. And some gardeners think you need a lot of plants to get any fruit. None of these ideas are correct.

In a perpetual fruit patch, the focus is on growing enough fruits for fresh eating throughout the growing season. This reduces the amount of space and time you need to grow fruit but increases the variety of fresh fruits you're able to grow. Unlike a berry farm or an orchard, we aren't looking to produce large quantities of fruit for sale, or even for freezing or canning. A perpetual fruit patch is all about eating fresh and seasonally, as the various fruits ripen. I was in the Peace Corps in Thailand in the 1980s, and I still clearly remember all the different fruits in the village market where I lived. Each month, I'd see a new fruit replace one that was no longer in season. It was exciting having such variety and a continuous supply of fruit to eat.

My wife and I now grow our fruits the very same way in our home garden. Starting with honeyberries in early summer (they mature two weeks before the strawberries) and then ending with pawpaws, figs, and persimmons in fall, we have fifteen different fruits maturing throughout the growing season. What's great is we don't need a lot of plants, or even large ones, to stay in fruit all summer and fall. Using dwarf and self-fertile varieties, we reduce both the space needed and the workload required to grow and care for our fruit patch. Less work and more fruit—I like that!

You can have the same experience in your own yard by planting fruits that mature in succession all summer and fall with the emphasis on growing only enough for fresh eating for your family. As in my yard, it will translate to fewer plants and less space, if you do it right. You'll also learn how to interplant fruit to further save space using the planting schemes I present later in this chapter.

With an explosion of interest in fruit growing, many gardeners are also interested in venturing beyond the classic apples, strawberries, and blueberries. That's great because you're about to learn how native and unusual fruits can also be part of the mix. Often these fruits are low-maintenance, hardy, and more compatible with native pollinators and other insects. Plus, they're often not found at your local farm stand or grocery store.

So, let's have some fun with fruits and dive into growing your own perpetual fruit patch.

HOW MUCH FRUIT DO YOU NEED?

A key to fruit growing is determining how much fruit you really need. At our home it's mostly my wife and I, so having an overabundance of fruit isn't necessary. We can plant a little of this and a little of that and achieve our goal of having fresh fruit throughout the season.

How much of each type of fruit to grow depends on a number of factors. How many people will be eating the fruit in your household? How much usable land do you have to grow fruit? Most fruit trees and berry bushes need at least a half day of sun to produce well. How much time do you want to spend caring for your fruit plants? Some fruits are relatively low-maintenance, while others may need pampering.

To give you an idea of how many plants of each fruit to grow, I created this chart of common fruits for a family of two and a family of four. Of course, the number of plants will also depend on how well the trees or bushes grow.

You can harvest a cornucopia of fruit even in a small yard.

Mixing and matching fruits with herbs and veggies allows you to maximize the space you have to garden.

FRUIT	TWO PEOPLE	FOUR PEOPLE
Apple	1–2 dwarf trees	2–3 dwarf trees
Blackberry	2–4 plants	4–6 plants
Blueberry	2 highbush plants	3–4 highbush plants
Cherry	1 dwarf self-fertile tree	2 dwarf trees
Currant/gooseberry	1 plant	2 plants
Fig	1 dwarf fig tree	1 dwarf fig tree
Grape	1–2 vines	3–4 vines
Honeyberry	2 plants for pollination	2–3 plants
Lemon/lime	1 dwarf tree	1 dwarf tree
Orange	1 dwarf tree	1 dwarf tree
Peach	1 tree	2 trees
Pear	1 tree	1 tree
Plum	1 self-fertile tree	2 trees
Raspberry	3–4 plants	4–6 plants
Strawberry	12–15 plants	25–30 plants

BEST BERRIES TO GROW IN THE PERPETUAL GARDEN

Probably the best place to start in the perpetual fruit garden is with berries. The bushes, plants, or vines are smaller than trees, making them easier to fit in the yard. Also, they produce fruits sooner than most tree fruits and, I believe, are generally easier to maintain.

To get you started with berries, I'm profiling my favorite—and the most popular—berries in this section. As I did with vegetables and herbs, I'm not going to give you all the information you need to grow these plants. That information is widely available on the internet and in fruit gardening books. Check out my resource section for further information. Instead, I will discuss the criteria that are important for a perpetual gardener. These include dwarf varieties, self-fertile varieties and disease-resistant varieties, types of fruits that fit into different places in your yard, and easy ways to maintain your berry plants.

Dwarf fruit trees and berry bushes pair well with vegetable beds.

BLUEBERRY (*VACCINIUM* SPP.)

I think the best perpetual berry for your efforts is the blueberry. The highbush blueberry produces an abundance of fruit per bush each year. If cared for well, they can produce for decades. Blueberries are generally grouped into highbush, half-high, and dwarf varieties.

LOCATION

Blueberries are handsome plants in the landscape. I encourage perpetual gardeners to plant them as foundation plants along their house or in gardens. I also encourage gardeners to plant at least two plants. It's best for pollination and you can extend the harvest by planting early, midseason, and late-season varieties. It's also easiest to protect them from hungry birds if they're grown together.

Highbush blueberries can grow 5 to 6 feet (1.5 to 1.8 m) tall and wide. If you only have a small space, consider growing half-high or dwarf berries such as 'Northcountry', 'Jelly Bean', and 'Perpetua'. Some of these varieties can be grown in containers as well. Bushel and Berry® features a line of dwarf berry bushes good for small spaces and container growing.

There are northern highbush blueberry varieties for cold areas and southern and rabbiteye varieties for the South. Wild variations, such as huckleberries and lowbush berries, are regional selections and are also fun to grow. Choose varieties based on your area.

GROW

Blueberries love full sun, well-drained and loose soil, and moisture. They also require acidic soil to grow best. Adjust the soil pH to be at or below 5.0. Add sulfur to lower your soil's pH, based on the soil test. Blueberries don't like heavy clay soil, so raise up the planting bed on clay soil by adding compost and organic materials. Blueberries love arborist's wood chips. Once I started mulching our plants with wood chips, their growth took off. Arborists wood chips are perfect because they're large and nonuniform in size. Water and air flows freely through them. Plus, they're often free. Check with your local arborist or with *getchipdrop.com* to get a load of chips. They break down slowly over time to feed the roots, and they keep the shallow roots moist and weed-free.

Nothing beats the flavor of fresh blueberries picked right off your own bush.

Protect blueberries from birds by covering them with netting before the fruits ripen.

MANAGING THE PLANTS

You can add compost or organic fertilizer to get your blueberries to grow faster, but in my experience, having healthy soil and mulching with organic materials works well.

Blueberries need little care for the first five or so years other than mulching, watering during dry times, and perhaps some fertilizing. You can always prune off dead growth or crossing branches each spring.

After year five, in spring, check the oldest branches (peeling gray bark) on your plants for fat, upright, flower buds. These will be obvious, in contrast, to the narrow leaf buds that are tucked along the stems. If the old stem has few flower buds, prune it back to a side branch or down to the ground to stimulate newer growth. A healthy blueberry should have at least five to seven strong, fruiting stems per plant.

Protect ripening blueberries from birds with netting. I erect a cage over my blueberries using 7-foot (2 m) tall, plastic-coated metal stakes with old tennis balls attached to the top. We simply slide bird netting over the poles and balls and anchor it to the ground with stakes or boards.

CURRANT AND GOOSEBERRY (*RIBES* SPP.)

Currants and gooseberries are underappreciated berry plants in the landscape, and they are perfect for a perpetual garden. Many varieties fruit the first year after planting and continue for multiple years. They only require occasional pruning, fertilizing with compost, and watering during droughts. While most gardeners are familiar with these fruits dried, canned, or juiced, I like them fresh for their tangy flavor.

Most currant and gooseberry plants only grow three to five feet (91 to 152 cm) tall and wide, making them perfect as foundation plants or small shrubs in a flower garden. I grow ours in an "edible hedgerow" that I'll describe in greater detail later in this chapter. Currants and gooseberries are self-fertile and can fruit in part-shade conditions. This opens up more possibilities for siting the plants.

You only need one plant to get fruit, but there are nice variations of both types so you might be tempted to plant more. Gooseberries can have green-colored fruits or deep red fruits, such as on the 'Red Hinnomaki' variety. Currants can be white ('White Imperial'), pink ('Pink Champagne'), red ('Jonkheer Van Tets'), or black ('Titania'). I particularly like the white, pink, and red gooseberries for fresh eating since they have a sweeter flavor. Black currants are usually used just for jam and juice making. The varieties mentioned here are all disease resistant.

Currants and gooseberries are not fussy about the soil. Well-drained soil is best, but ours grow on clay and seem fine. Once established, there's little to do to keep them happy other than annual additions of compost and mulch.

'Red Hinnomaki' gooseberry is surprisingly sweet.

Currants can be eaten fresh off the bush or used for making jam or juice.

MANAGING THE PLANTS

Currants and gooseberries can get diseases that not only affect the plants but also other plants near them. Always look for disease-resistant varieties to prevent the spread of white pine blister rust (a fungal disease that is hosted on currants and gooseberries). Other varieties may get powdery mildew midseason that will defoliate the plant, making them less attractive in the landscape. The currant worm can also attack plants but is easily controlled in early summer with an organic spray.

The most maintenance you'll need to do with these bushes is annual pruning. Leave the plants unpruned until they're four years old, then prune out the oldest canes to the ground. Currants and gooseberries fruit best on one-to-three-year-old canes. Repeat this pruning annually. You should still have nine to twelve canes of varying ages per mature bush.

GRAPE (*VITIS* SPP.)

Many gardeners shy away from grape growing because they feel they need a large area to grow these vines. While this may be true if you're trying to make wine, for fresh eating you only need a few vines. You also have the option of growing them on a pergola, fence, or arbor.

Fresh, seedless table grapes are delicious, and I have some favorite varieties that grow well even in our cold New England climate. 'Somerset Red Seedless' is a small-sized, hardy, seedless variety that produces fruit annually in abundance. Other good northern seedless varieties include 'Canadice' (red), 'Everest' (blue) and 'Himrod' (white). Some varieties for the South are 'Jupiter' (blue), 'Compassion' (white), and 'Tickled Pink' (pink). For the West, try 'Thompson Seedless' (white), 'Flame Seedless' (red), and 'Crimson Seedless' (red).

For a small family, you may only need 3 to 4 vines spaced 5 feet (1.5 m) apart. You can grow them on a wire fence simply made with wooden or metal posts with a metal wire strung between them. Grapevines are perfect placed on the edge of the yard. They can double as a boundary marker for your property line.

You can also trellis grapevines up a wall or the side of a building. This can really save space. However, keep the plants away from any wooden structures to prevent the siding from rotting. Another use for grapevines is to provide shade. If you have an arbor or pergola, you can grow grapevines up the posts and have them cover the top, providing summer shade.

Grapes grow well in many soils but don't like poorly drained soils. They actually grow, and the fruits taste better, in soils with average or even below average fertility. They grow best in full sun, but you'll still get some production in part shade. Growing in an airy location is great to reduce disease issues. Grapes will bear fruit a few years after planting. Use a netting system, similar to what I described for blueberries, to keep birds away.

You only need a few vines to yield plenty of table grapes for fresh eating.

Prune grapes in late winter, removing 70 percent of the vine.

MANAGING THE PLANTS

Probably the biggest chores with grape growing is setting up a trellis, fence, or structure for them to grow on and pruning.

To prune table grapes on a single wire fence, let the vine grow straight up on a stake the first year. Once it reaches the wire, cut the tip of the vine off to stimulate side branching. Train one side branch on either side of the main trunk on the wire. Each year after that, remove the old fruiting shoots and errant shoots and save two new shoots on each side of the trunk. Remove up to 70 percent of the shoots each year. Prune these shoots to ten to twenty buds and attach them to the wire. These are the fruiting arms for that same year.

On a pergola, let the vine grow up to the top of the structure. Top the vine to stimulate side branching and select four stems (arms). Shorten them to 5 feet (1.5 m) long and tie them to the structure. Each year allow four shoots to form off of each arm. Prune those shoots to eight to twelve buds on each. These are your fruiting shoots for that same year.

HONEYBERRY (*LONICERA CAERULEA*)

Honeyberries are not as well known as the other berries I discuss in this chapter, but I love them and think they have a bright future in a perpetual garden. Honeyberry is in the honeysuckle family. Its origin is Siberia, so it's very hardy and tough. While it can grow in northern areas of Canada, Russia, and Japan well, it also can grow in slightly warmer climates. Unlike some of the invasive species of honeysuckle, this plant does not spread aggressively.

The dark purple, elongated, small berries are produced two weeks before strawberries, making this plant the earliest producer of all of our berry bushes. The fruits are loaded with antioxidants and have a blackberrylike or grapelike flavor. We use them in fruit shakes, yogurt, and salads. For the sweetest flavor, let them fully mature on the bush so they're dropping off the plant. In fact, that's the best way to harvest honeyberries. Place an old bed sheet under the plant and shake it. The ripe berries will drop onto the sheet.

There are increasingly more varieties available as people discover honeyberries. I grow 'Blue Moon', 'Blue Velvet', and 'Borealis'. The plants stay a compact 3 feet (91 cm) tall and a bit wider. It's best to have two different varieties for pollination and fruit set.

Since honeyberry bushes tend to be small and compact, they make great plants for a foundation planting along a building or in a flower or vegetable garden. The fruits are produced early and, for the rest of the year, the blue-green leaves are an attractive backdrop to other plants and flowers.

For the best berry production, grow honeyberry bushes in full sun in well-drained, compost-rich soil. I first purchased honeyberry plants through the mail years ago. I received two small "sticks" and thought I'd been had. But those "sticks" grew into 1-foot (30 cm)-tall-and-wide bushes the first year and doubled in size the second year, producing fruits, too.

Honeyberry fruits form in abundance along the stems about two weeks before strawberries ripen.

Honeyberries have a rich, slightly start flavor and are loaded with antioxidants.

MANAGING THE PLANTS

Honeyberries have few insect pests, and deer and rabbits don't seem to bother them. They don't need much attention other than some compost and a little pruning in spring. Mine have produced berries consistently each year.

Once mature, I thin out the centers of the bushes in spring to open up crowded areas and provide more airflow. But honestly, I think if I did nothing, they still would produce.

Birds can clean out a bush quickly, so once you see the fruits starting to turn purple, drape bird netting over the shrubs. We cover the bushes to get a few good harvests, then share the rest with the birds. It's a great early season food source for them.

RASPBERRY AND BLACKBERRY (*RUBUS* SPP.)

Some of the easiest berry plants to grow have to be in the *Rubus* family. These include raspberries and blackberries. Blackberries, in particular, have a fond place in my heart. I grew up with wild blackberries on my grandfather's farm and remember many summer days when my cousins and I would go pick and eat blackberries until our faces were purple and our arms were covered with scratches from the thorns.

Raspberries and blackberries fit nicely in many locations in a perpetual garden. They will produce fruit even in a part-shade spot, and once established, they tend to grow well for years.

Red or yellow raspberry and blackberry roots will spread, so place them where it's easy to keep them in bounds. I find along the side of a garage, house, or shed is perfect. The building blocks the roots' spreading in one direction, and if you have lawn on the other side, then the mowing stops it in the other direction. I have my brambles planted in rows in the middle of a meadow that gets mowed every month or so instead of weekly like the lawn. This helps me keep up with errant blackberry and raspberry shoots.

There are also clumping versions of raspberries, such as purple raspberries and black raspberries. These are also favorites of mine. Although they will spread a bit by underground rhizomes, for the most part they stay in a clump, making them a nice choice for small-space gardens. I've even seen these plants grown in the back of a flower border because they stay tame.

Blackberries produce abundantly and you can now purchase thornless varieties which make harvesting easier.

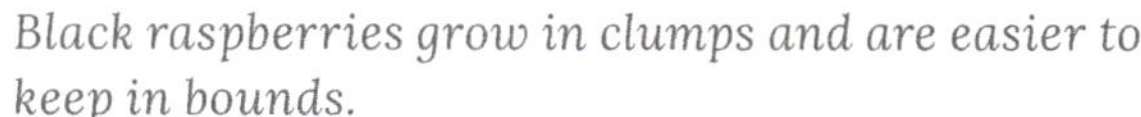

Black raspberries grow in clumps and are easier to keep in bounds.

GROW

There are many varieties of raspberries for a home gardener to grow. Choose varieties adapted to your local region. Red raspberry varieties include 'Boyne' and 'Encore'. 'Cascade Gold' is a yellow-fruited variety. 'Blackhawk' is the black raspberry variety I grow and 'Royalty' is a purple raspberry variety.

For blackberries, I grow 'Nelson' because it's adapted to our climate. For other regions, try 'Navaho' and 'Natchez' in hot, humid climates. They're thornless and hardy to -10°F (-23°C). For wetter climates, try 'Triple Crown Thornless'. It's hardy to -20°F (-29°C) and is productive and tasty. 'Columbia Giant' is a large-fruited, thornless, trailing type that is hardy to -10°F (-23°C).

Both raspberries and blackberries also have everbearing varieties that bear two crops in one year. Most typical raspberry and blackberry varieties bear fruit only in the summer on two-year-old canes. The first year the primocanes grow vertically and overwinter, then flower and fruit the summer of the second year (now they're called the floricanes). Everbearing varieties flower and fruit on the primocanes *and* the floricanes, so they fruit once in summer (floricane) and once in fall (primocane). 'Caroline' and 'Polana' are good, red, everbearing varieties. 'Ann' and 'Fall Gold' are good, yellow-fruited, everbearing varieties.

The University of Arkansas has produced many varieties of everbearing blackberries, such as 'Prime Ark® Traveler' and 'Prime Ark® Freedom'. They're also thornless. There are even dwarf varieties that can grow in containers such as 'Baby Cakes' blackberry and 'Raspberry Shortcake' red raspberry.

There are also many crosses of blackberries and raspberries that offer different-sized fruits with sweet and tangy flavors. Loganberry, marionberry, dewberry, olallieberry, and boysenberry are just some of these crosses.

MANAGING THE PLANTS

The key to keeping raspberries and blackberries manageable is trellising and pruning. Raspberries, and some blackberries, have erect canes that don't trail and droop. It's easier to keep the canes upright and they won't sprawl as much.

Some blackberries have trailing canes that are more flexible and need to be supported to stay vertical. They require more handling.

Trellis erect types of raspberries and blackberries on wire strung between wooden or metal posts. Erect varieties have stiff canes and only need wire stretched on either side of the bed, 3 to 4 feet (91 to 122 cm) off the ground, between two *T* posts on the ends of the bed. Trailing blackberry varieties have weaker canes and are best trellised with two wires. One wire should be at a height of 3 feet (91 cm) and another at a height of 5 feet (1.5 m). In late summer, as the primocanes grow, loop bundles of canes around the wires in both directions. In colder areas, leave the bundles of canes on the ground to be protected by snow or mulch. Come spring, loop them around the wires.

STRAWBERRY (*FRAGARIA* SPP.)

Strawberries are one of those delightful summer crops gardeners can't wait to eat. The soft, sweet, warm berries have a hard time making it into the kitchen because they often are eaten before they reach the door.

Most gardeners know of the June-bearing strawberries found at pick-your-own farms. These varieties produce lots of fruit all at once and then create new plants by runners that spread around the vicinity. But, there are other types of strawberries that fit well in the continuous vegetable garden. Day-neutral varieties don't send out many runners (it's recommended to remove the runners as they form). This means the plant will send more energy into fruit production and less into new plant growth. Alpine and wild strawberries have small plants and fruits. They spread quickly to fill an area, but their small leaves tend not to crowd out nearby flowers and herbs. Their small fruits come in colors such as red, yellow, and white, and they have a delightful taste. Alpine and wild strawberries produce fruit all summer.

Some good June-bearing strawberry varieties include 'Sparkle' and 'Jewel'. It's good to plant early, midseason, and late-season varieties to extend the harvest a few more weeks. Some day-neutral varieties are 'Tribute' and 'Seascape'. Always look for disease-resistant varieties adapted to your area.

I first realized strawberries make great ground covers when some plants escaped from our strawberry patch and found their way under some fruit trees. They happily spread around the trees until I found them. Instead of digging them out, I embraced their ingenuity and started encouraging strawberries in other parts of our yard—partly because strawberries reproduce so well and also because they make excellent ground covers, particularly around trees and shrubs.

Now I have strawberries everywhere. I planted June-bearing strawberries under shrubs in our edible hedgerow, in tree rings around fruit trees in our yard instead of using wood mulch, and even in some flower gardens with tough, large perennials such as peonies.

Alpine strawberries are nice in the herb garden and gardens with smaller flowers. Even though they spread, the leaves are smaller than June-bearing and day-neutral types, so they are less likely to crowd out other flowers and herbs.

For a perpetual gardener with limited space, grow day-neutral varieties. They produce fruits all summer in small quantities (versus June bearers that produce fruit all at once in large quantities). This is perfect for fresh eating every day. Day-neutral varieties also don't spread as aggressively by runners as June bearers, and if you remove most of the runners as they form, you'll get more berries.

Strawberries make great container plants. Choose day neutral varieties that will fruit all summer.

Strawberries are good ground covers in our garden. They cover the soil, keeping it cool and moist and we (and the birds) get the benefit of eating the berries.

GROW

Strawberries grow best in full sun in light, well-drained soil. Raised beds are perfect for strawberry growing. Heavy, wet soils will kill the roots. Amend the soil with compost.

June-bearing plants will not fruit the first year. Even if they start forming flowers, it's recommended to remove the blooms so the plant puts more energy into growing roots. Day-neutral and alpine strawberry plants also have the recommendation to remove the flowers after planting, but only until July 1. Then you can let the flowers set and form fruits to eat in late summer and fall.

MANAGING THE PLANTS

For June-bearing strawberry varieties, allow the plants to set runners and fill in the bed after harvest. In late summer, remove overcrowded plants, favoring younger plants. The spacing will help the plants fruit better next year. Cover the strawberry bed with hay or straw in fall in cold climates to prevent the plants from heaving out of the ground due to the freezing soil. For my ground cover strawberries, I don't bother with thinning. They produce less berries, but there are so many plants, we have plenty to eat.

For day-neutral varieties, if you remove all the runners, then you'll just have the original plant the next year. After a few years you may have to replace these day-neutral plants due to diseases. To get around this, leave some runners to form in late summer and these can become your replacement plants for the coming years.

THE BEST TREE FRUITS TO GROW IN THE PERPETUAL GARDEN

Fruit trees may seem like a luxury or an impossible fit in a smaller perpetual garden, but you'll be surprised to see how well they work. Many fruit tree varieties are self-fertile, meaning you only need one tree to get fruit. With modern breeding and grafting, there are more dwarf varieties than ever too. And if you're up for a challenge, you can use certain pruning techniques to keep fruit trees a manageable size and still productive.

There is much information available online and in books about growing fruit trees, the best varieties for your region, and how to care for them. Check my resource section in the back of this book for more information. Here, I'm emphasizing dwarf, self-fertile, disease-resistant varieties whenever I can and focusing on how they could work in a perpetual vegetable gardener's yard.

Many new apple varieties come as dwarf trees which makes harvesting a snap.

Mint is grown under some of our trees as a ground cover and herb for eating

APPLE (*MALUS DOMESTICA*)

If you think that fitting an apple tree in your small, perpetual vegetable garden is impossible, think again. The trend for fruit trees is to "get small." With apples, you can now grow dwarf trees that start producing fruit in a few years and are disease resistant and attractive in your yard.

Choose apple tree varieties that grow more vertical with fewer side branches.

Dwarf apple varieties that only grow 8 to 15-feet (2.4 to 4.6 m) tall and are self-fertile include 'Jon A Red', 'Dwarf Gala', and 'Dwarf Liberty'. While some apple varieties are self-fertile, they always can benefit from having another variety around that blooms at the same time. Look for regional varieties that are adapted to your climate. For example, in regions that have mild winters, look for low-chill varieties that don't need a cold winter to flower and fruit properly, such as 'Anna' and 'Dorsett Golden'.

Another unique apple type is the columnar apple tree. This fascinating variety grows about 8 feet (2.4 m) tall, with only short, stubby, fruiting spurs and a single upright trunk. The fruits form on the fruiting spurs along the main trunk. Columnar is a good word to describe their look. You won't get a tremendous yield compared to other apple varieties, but they are perfect for a perpetual gardener who wants a modest harvest of fresh apples. Plus, since they're so vertical, it's easy to find space for them in the yard.

Finally, espalier is a technique where trees are pruned on a single plane, usually against a wall or fence. The branches can run horizontal, away from the trunk, or radiate upward in a form called a Belgian fence. While espalier requires more complex pruning and growing techniques, nurseries now offer pre-pruned espalier fruit trees that take much of the hard work out of creating the tree's structure. You'll find apples, pears, peaches, and other fruit trees now pruned in an espalier form in nurseries.

LOCATION

Most gardeners think of planting an apple tree in the lawn or along the edge of their property. But with dwarf varieties, you have more options.

Columnar apple trees are easily tucked into a vegetable or flower garden. Because they stand tall with little side branching, there's not much shading around them, so you can still grow all types of vegetables, herbs, and flowers nearby.

You can also use apple trees as ornamental trees in your lawn, substituting them for ornamental crabapple, redbud, flowering cherry, and other decorative trees. You'll get the same flower show in spring, but then you'll also get fruit in summer and fall.

GROW

Apple trees grow best in full sun in well-drained, fertile soils. This is especially important for dwarf varieties, which don't have as strong a root system as semi-dwarf and standard-sized trees. Fertilizing in spring with compost and an organic fruit tree fertilizer can help get them established.

Plant apple trees at the proper depth. Dwarf trees tend to be grafted. The rootstock, or bottom portion, has the dwarfing characteristic you want. If you bury the graft union (the bulge on the tree near the bottom of the trunk), you may lose the dwarfing effect. Always leave the graft union above the soil line.

MANAGING THE TREE

Dwarf trees inherently need less care. In winter, prune apple trees to remove dead, diseased, and broken branches. Dwarf trees may need some pruning to open the center, remove suckers and water sprout branches, and reduce shading or overcrowded branches.

By selecting a disease-resistant variety, such as 'MacFree', there's little need for spraying your apple trees. For common insects, such as codling moth and apple maggots, there are traps you can hang from the trees to lure and catch them. The traps may not get all the bad insects, but you still should get a good-looking crop of apples.

The one downside of dwarf fruit trees is their longevity. Dwarf trees just aren't strong enough to live as long as a standard-sized apple tree. But the pleasure you get from your dwarf tree will come sooner.

CHERRY (*PRUNUS AVIUM* AND *P. CERASUS*)

Cherries are an easy-to-grow, perpetual fruit garden tree because they are relatively small and there are self-fertile varieties. Plus, why grow an ornamental cherry tree for its spring flowers, when an edible type looks just as beautiful!

Cherries are grouped into two types: sweet and tart. Sweet cherry varieties are delicious eaten fresh but are less cold tolerant compared to tart varieties. Tart varieties are mostly used in cooking, jam and pie making, but there are varieties I think taste good eaten fresh as well. Tart cherry trees are longer lived and tougher trees, especially in cold climates. Most sweet cherries are hardy to -20F (-29°C), while most tart cherries can survive down to -30°F (-34°C).

For sweet cherry varieties, try the self-fertile 'Lapins', 'Stella', and 'Sweetheart' varieties. You can select dwarf versions that grow around 12 feet (3.7 m) tall. Nearly all tart cherry varieties are self-fertile. Our favorite is 'Dwarf Northstar'. It only grows 8 to 10 feet (2.4 to 3 m) tall and produces consistent crops of bright red fruits. Other good tart cherry varieties include 'Meteor' and 'Montmorency'.

By selecting dwarf trees, you'll have many options in terms of where to plant them. Since they have beautiful spring flowers, consider planting cherries in the front yard. This will save space for other plantings. You also can create a small, part-shade garden by planting a cherry tree and growing part-shade–loving flowers, edibles, and herbs under the tree. I grow alpine strawberries and mint under our cherry trees.

Cherry trees grow best in full sun and in well-drained soil. Like all stone fruits, cherries don't grow well in heavy clay and wet soils. Consider raising up the soil if you're planting in those conditions. Add compost around the young trees and protect the trunk's bark from rabbits and mice in winter.

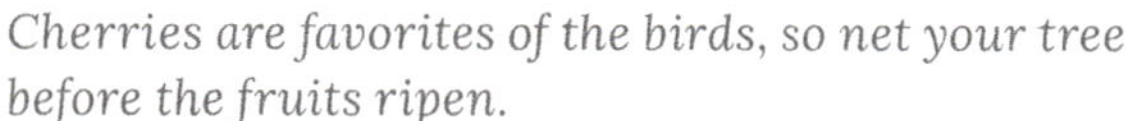

Cherries are favorites of the birds, so net your tree before the fruits ripen.

Cherry trees have attractive white flowers in spring.

MANAGING THE TREE

Cherry trees don't require a lot of maintenance and work. Dwarf trees are lightly pruned in spring to remove dead, diseased, and broken branches, crossing or rubbing branches, and to open up the canopy for better light penetration.

Well-drained soil will help prevent root rot diseases. There are some insect pests on cherries, but for a home gardener, it's usually not a significant problem. However, birds love cherries. I create a netting box over our dwarf trees (see photo above) that allows us to get inside the netting to harvest but keeps our feathered friends away.

CITRUS (*CITRUS* SPP.)

Citrus trees can be very rewarding. You'll get more fruit than you will need per tree, and the fruits will mature slowly, over time, making them perfect for the perpetual gardener who just wants fruits when they need them.

The downside of growing citrus is that most citrus trees are only hardy where winters don't dip below 10°F (-12°C) and warmer is better. But there are many dwarf varieties of various citrus that can be grown in containers and moved indoors in winter in colder areas.

Whether you're growing citrus in the ground outdoors or in containers, it makes sense to grow dwarf varieties. Some of the best types for home gardeners include 'Improved Meyer' lemon, 'Calamondin' orange, 'Bearss' lime, kumquats, and 'Clementine' mandarin orange. Always buy nursery-grown trees. These trees are grafted and will start fruiting in a few years. Starting citrus from seed is fun, but the trees will take longer to flower and fruit or may not fruit at all.

In warm climates, grow citrus trees and bushes along the edge of your property or create a little citrus grove, grouping them together in an island. In cold areas, grow citrus in large containers and move them outdoors in summer to a sunny patio, deck, or balcony that's protected from strong winds. The nice thing about container citrus in any climate is the trees stay short (6 feet [1.8 m]), and you can move the plants to protect them from adverse weather. Of course, you'll need a protected, bright, indoor space in winter to grow these evergreens.

Citrus grow best in full sun in well-drained, slightly acidic soils. In marginally hardy areas, protect trees once the fall temperatures start to drop to 50°F (10°C). Bring container citrus indoors at that time.

Water citrus when the soil dries out. Water deeply and infrequently. Too much water, especially in containers, can cause leaf drop. Fertilize with citrus plant food monthly only during the growing season. Let the plants rest in winter.

Who doesn't love picking fresh lemons off your own tree?

MANAGING THE TREE

Citrus need little pruning other than to remove dead, diseased, and broken branches. Many types of citrus will have flowers and maturing fruit on the tree at the same time. Harvest the fruit when they turn the mature color for that variety. Taste testing for ripeness is fine as well. Lemons and limes may continue flowering indoors in winter if they have enough light.

Watch for mealybugs and scale on citrus trees, especially trees in pots that are brought indoors. Spray with neem oil to control these pests.

FIG (*FICUS CARICA*)

I first fell in love with fresh figs in California. Then I realized I could grow them even in Vermont. We've been enjoying our own fresh figs ever since.

Fig trees are hardy down to about 0°F (-18°C) and perhaps colder with winter protection. Where they grow naturally, they can become 30-foot (9.1 m)-tall trees, loaded with fruit that actually becomes a nuisance when it drops and rots. For the continuous vegetable gardener, it's best to choose dwarf varieties or grow figs in containers. Most figs are self-fertile, so you only need one tree to get figs. The container naturally dwarfs trees, giving you more flexibility when growing them in your yard.

Some good dwarf varieties to grow in the ground in warm areas include 'Petit Negri' and 'Violeta de Bourdeaux', which grow only 10 feet (3 m) tall. 'Fignomenal' is touted as only growing a few feet (about 1 m) tall.

Some fig varieties are also great container plants. I grow 'Brown Turkey', 'Hardy Chicago', and 'Celeste' in containers, and they have produced for years.

Fig trees produce an abundance of fruits mostly in late summer.

Containers keep fig trees short and easy to move, and protect them in cold climates.

LOCATION

A full-sized fig tree in your yard can take up the whole space. Plant dwarf varieties in a hedgerow mixed with fruits, in the back of a sunny flower border, or on the north side of the vegetable garden so the tree won't shade your veggies. If you're growing vegetables, such as greens, that need some midsummer shade, then your fig tree, with its large leaves, can provide it. Fig trees growing in containers can give an elegant look to a patio or garden.

GROW

Figs grow best in full sun in well-drained soil. Figs like the heat. If you're growing them in a marginally hardy area, find a south- or west-facing wall building side, or hedge to plant them in front of and create a microclimate. This will help the plant overwinter and produce figs faster in summer.

I grow some figs in containers and some in our unheated greenhouse. The 'Hardy Chicago' fig in our greenhouse can survive our -20°F (-29°C) winters with some help. In fall, I cut back the main stems to a couple of feet (about 1 m) off the ground and wrap them with winter-weight row cover. Between the greenhouse glazing and the row covers, the stems survive each winter and grow into fruit-producing stems the next year. While you can get an early crop of figs off the old branches, most fig fruits form on new growth that forms in spring.

Container figs should be allowed to drop their leaves and go dormant in fall. Before the temperatures dip below 30°F (-1°C), move the containers to a protected spot for winter where the temperatures stay ideally just above freezing.

MANAGING THE TREE

Figs can be severely pruned and will still produce fruit. Prune in late winter before the leaves form. For container figs, root pruning is also a good idea. When you bring your fig containers out of winter storage, pop the root ball out of the pot. Trim off a few inches (about 8 cm) of roots all around the root ball then repot the tree into the same container with a mix of fresh potting soil, compost, and some organic fertilizer.

Keep fig trees well watered all summer, especially once fruiting starts in late summer. I've had container figs accidentally dry out and drop all their unripe fruit. Look for a color and texture change on your figs to know when to harvest.

PEACH (*PRUNUS PERSICA*)

There's nothing more delicious than a sun-warmed, ripe peach right off the tree. Peaches naturally aren't large trees, only growing about 15 feet (4.6 m) tall, but it's still good to plant dwarf varieties. Some good, genetic dwarf peaches that grow only 6 feet (1.8 m) tall include 'El Dorado', 'Pix Zee Dwarf', and 'Bonanza'. These varieties are hardy to about -10°F (-23°C). Many other varieties are hardy to -20°F (-29°C). Dwarf peach trees also grow well in containers.

My Italian relatives always had a peach tree or two growing in their vegetable garden. They would keep the size manageable by pruning. They got peaches, but the tree didn't interfere with their tomatoes and other veggies. Plant them on the north side of the garden to avoid shading sun-loving edibles. Peaches are also good to plant mixed with other tree fruits in a hedgerow or along a property boundary.

Peaches grow best in full sun in well-drained soil. Like all stone fruits, peaches don't like clay soils with poor drainage. Amend the soil with compost and fertilize with an organic plant food if the new growth isn't at least 1 foot (30 cm) long. Once fruiting starts, the new growth can be shorter. Keep your trees well watered and mulched.

Peaches grow fast and start fruiting a few years after planting. Only let a few fruits mature in the early years until the tree is large enough to support a bigger crop. Also, thin the young peaches heavily in early summer when they are the size of the quarter. Thin the fruits to 6 inches (15 cm) apart to reduce the fruit load and prevent branches from breaking.

Prune in late winter to a vase shape to keep the tree open, allowing light to penetrate to the center. Remove dead, diseased, and broken branches any time.

Nothing beats the taste of a warm, mature peach freshly harvested off your tree. Harvest peaches when the background skin color changes from green to tan and the fruit is still firm.

MANAGING THE TREE

Control peach leaf curl disease by spraying copper sulfate in late winter. Or grow peach leaf curl-resistant varieties such as 'Frost'. Keep the trunk healthy and watch for peach borers. If you discover borer holes, stick a metal wire into their small holes in the trunk to kill the tunneling larvae.

Harvest peaches once the background color of the fruit turns from green to light tan. Harvest a little earlier to avoid bird and animal damage. Mature fruit will continue to ripen in a warm room.

PEAR (*PYRUS COMMUNIS*)

Pears are a fall treat in our garden. Pear trees tend to grow large and tall. They start fruiting three to five years after planting and can last for decades. Luckily, there are semi-dwarf and dwarf versions of many of the common European varieties such as 'Bartlett', 'Bosc', and 'Comice' that only grow 15 feet (4.6 m) tall. I grow Asian pears, too. Some varieties, such as 'Shinseiki' and 'Chojuro', also stay short.

Normally, you need two pear varieties to get the best pollination. I grow 'Summercrisp' and 'Luscious' with good success. Check European and Asian pear varieties for good pollinator buddies. Many varieties are hardy to -20°F (-29°C) or even colder.

Since these are larger fruit trees than the ones I've mentioned so far, plant pears away from gardens such as along a property boundary line or in a hedgerow. The one advantage these fruit trees have over others is that pears like to naturally grow vertically and narrow. This allows other plants to grow nearby without being shaded out. Pears also can be pruned into espalier trees. However, pears are not great container trees.

Like apples, pears can tolerate clay-based, wet soils better than any of the stone crop fruits. But pears will grow better in well-drained soil. Full sun is important for flowering and fruiting. One reason pears sometimes don't fruit well is poor pollination. Pear nectar has only about 10 percent sugar, compared to apple nectar with 50 percent sugar, so the flowers are not as attractive to bees. Plant at least two different varieties that are compatible for pollination. Add compost and mulch annually. Keep well watered when young, especially during dry periods.

Pears are best harvested before they fully ripen on the tree and are still firm. Harvest pears when they easily separate from the branch. To check, gently lift and tilt the fruit upwards. It should easily separate.

MANAGING THE TREE

Pears only require light pruning to remove dead, diseased, and broken branches and to encourage the branch crotch angles to be wider. Some varieties of pears are better at growing wider crotch angles than others. Pruning can only do so much when genetics is involved. I like growing European pears that are disease resistant, especially from fire blight disease.

Harvest pears when the dark green skin color turns a lighter green or yellow green. The texture should still be firm. Don't allow pears to fully ripen on the tree and get soft, or the fruit center will be overripe. Harvest Asian pears when the fruit easily slips off the branch when lifted and turned.

PLUM (*PRUNUS DOMESTICA*)

Plums are great for snacking. The fruits tend to be small, so it's easy to eat a handful just standing next to the tree. I do it all the time! They're great for kids in that regard, too. There are three main types of plums. American hybrids, such as 'Toka' and 'Waneta' are the hardiest. European varieties, such as 'Mount Royal', 'Green Gage', and 'Superior', are some of the most flavorful plums. Japanese varieties, such as 'Shiro' and 'Santa Rosa', are best in warmer climates.

Most plums need two varieties within the same plum type for pollination. Luckily, plum trees tend to be small (less than 16 feet [4.9 m] tall), so planting more than one tree may work depending on your yard size. Some varieties, such as 'Santa Rose', 'Stanley', and 'Damson', will set fruit with just one tree, but you'll still get more fruit with a pollinator tree nearby. Always look for disease-resistant varieties when possible.

Plums naturally like to form thickets of trees, so I've spaced my trees a bit closer together (8 feet [2.4 m]) than what's recommended to create what I call a "plum village." The trees create a canopy of plums in a small space. This is especially easy to do with dwarf varieties.

You can plant plums on the north side of your vegetable garden, as a backdrop in a flower garden, or with other fruits in a hedgerow or island planting. Wild plums are particularly suited to naturalized plantings.

Plums grow best with full sun in an airy, open area. This helps reduce diseases, such as black knot, from taking hold. Like cherries and peaches, plums need well-drained soil and don't grow well in clay.

The trees are fast growing and start fruiting a few years after planting. Like peaches, your tree branches should be growing 12 inches (30 cm) a year until fruiting occurs when the new growth can be less. Add compost and organic fruit tree fertilizer as needed.

Plum trees come in many different varieties for different climates.

Once mature, plum trees tend to overproduce. It's best to thin the fruits, spacing them 4 inches (10 cm) apart, when they're the size of a US quarter. This will improve the quality of the main crop and reduce the likelihood of branches cracking due to the fruits' weight. This also prevents alternate bearing, where trees take a year off from fruiting after a heavy crop the previous year.

Prune plums to open the center of the tree for better light penetration, flowering, and fruiting. Remove dead, diseased, and broken branches and, in late winter, remove crossing or rubbing branches. This also will help prevent diseases. Prune out branches with black knot disease at any time.

Lessen plum curculio insects by picking up and discarding dropped fruit, spraying kaolin clay on the trees after fruit set, and even letting chickens roam under your trees to eat the insects.

Harvest when the fruits turn the right color for that variety and come off the tree easily with a gentle tug.

EXPERIMENT WITH NATIVE FRUITS

The traditional types of berries and tree fruits discussed through the first part of this chapter are great in a perpetual fruit garden, but there are good reasons to grow native fruits too. Native plants are better adapted to your climate, soil, insects and wildlife, and sun conditions. They also tend to have fewer problems with diseases, insects, and animal damage.

Native fruit-bearing species can be very regional so check local resources to find the best native fruit bushes and trees for your region. I'm going to highlight some of my favorites that are adapted to broad sections of North America. Most of these natives are good for fresh eating as well as processing.

PLANT PROFILE

SERVICEBERRY, SASKATOON, JUNEBERRY (*AMELANCHIER CANADENSIS* AND *A. ALNIFOLIA*)

Serviceberries and saskatoons are small trees or large shrubs. They're native to Canada and the United States. There are many varieties of serviceberry that are mostly used as landscape plants for their ornamental flowers and fall color. Lesser known are the blue berries that form after flowering. They mostly get overlooked because birds love them and will clean out a tree in hours.

The large bush version of serviceberry is called a saskatoon, named after the Canadian town. Canada has a thriving saskatoon-farming industry. Saskatoons have a smaller plant, but larger berries than other serviceberries. Varieties, such as 'Regent', 'Thiessen', and 'Smoky', mature in early summer with tasty berries. They can be eaten fresh or made into jams, jellies, or juice. Saskatoon berries have a sweet, nutty flavor and are high in antioxidants.

Serviceberry trees are beautiful ornamental trees in the landscape and have the bonus of producing tasty fruits.

GROW

Serviceberries are trouble-free, easy to grow, and have colorful fall foliage. That's the reason landscapers like them so much. When planting a saskatoon variety for berry production, plant in full sun in well-drained soil. Mulch around the tree to protect the shallow roots from competition with grass and weeds. Keep well watered the first year and fertilize only with compost. After the plant gets established, it won't need much attention.

It will take three to five years for serviceberries and saskatoons to start producing berries. Protect the plants, as you would blueberries, from birds with netting.

AMERICAN PERSIMMON (*DIOSPYROS VIRGINIANA*)

Many gardeners may be familiar with the Asian persimmon (*D. kaki*). This 0°F (-18°C)-hardy tree is popular in California and warmer regions of the United States. While the Asian persimmon is native to East Asia and India, there is an American version (hardy to -20°F [-29°C]) that's native from New England to Florida and west to Kansas and Texas.

The American persimmon has fruits that need to be very ripe before being eaten fresh. Otherwise, the flavor is very astringent. The orange- or yellow-colored fruits are a handball size and ripen in late fall. You only need one tree to get fruits. There are named varieties that produce better-quality fruit than the straight species. Look for 'Meader', 'Prok', 'John Rick', and 'Early Golden' as some of the most widely available varieties. There are some crosses with the Asian persimmons, such as 'Nikita's Gift', that feature larger-sized fruits with better flavor on more cold-tolerant trees. The texture of the American persimmon ripe fruit is creamy, like a custard. The flavor is complex with hints of honey, dates, and caramel.

GROW

Plant the American persimmon trees in full sun to get the best production. They thrive in well-drained, fertile soils. Once established, they're low-maintenance trees. The trees have a tropical look with large, avocado-like leaves. The leaves turn a golden color in fall and often drop while the orange-colored fruits are still on the trees. This gives the tree a spooky appearance in October.

American persimmon fruits are harvested in fall when still hard but fully colored. You can finish ripening them indoors. They can also ripen on the tree but may be harder to harvest without damaging the soft, ripe fruits. Harvesting early helps prevent animals, such as raccoons, from stealing the harvest. However, the trees are usually so productive, you'll be happy to share the bounty with wildlife.

You only need one American persimmon tree to get a ton of luscious fruits.

American persimmon fruits will hang on the tree after the leaves drop in fall.

PAWPAW (*ASIMINA TRILOBA*)

This unusual American fruit is native in North America from New England to Georgia and west to the Mississippi River and is hardy to -20°F (-29°C). It's the only temperate climate version of the tropical cherimoya fruit. And it looks it! It grows up to 25 feet (7.6 m) tall in a pyramid shape with large, avocado-like leaves.

The fruits are mango-shaped and form in clusters. They ripen in fall and have a golden flesh color. The texture is custardy, and the taste is like a mix between a banana, mango, and papaya.

The popularity of pawpaws is growing. Some newer varieties to include in your continuous vegetable garden are 'Sunshine', 'Susquehanna', 'Shenandoah', and 'Zimmerman'. You'll need two different varieties to get good pollination and fruit set. Trees start bearing when they are 3 to 4 years old.

Pawpaw fruits look like they belong in the tropics, but they are hardy North American native plants.

GROW

Pawpaw trees grow as an understory tree in thickets in the wild. Young trees like shade, but older trees fruit best in full sun. So, protect younger trees from the harsh afternoon sun.

Pawpaw flowers are notoriously hard to pollinate. Native insects just aren't that interested in them. They bloom later than other fruit trees so often aren't bothered by a late frost. To ensure a good crop, I go out in the morning when the flowers are open to hand-pollinate the flowers using a cotton swab or small paintbrush. It's quick and effective.

The trees need little pruning other than removing dead, diseased, and broken branches. Protect the tender bark from rodents and rabbits in winter.

Harvest the fruits when they turn soft to the touch and start changing to a pale yellow skin color. Remove the seeds and eat the fruits fresh, make shakes and ice cream, or bake with them.

Pawpaw fruits have delicious yellow flesh that's great eaten fresh and made into ice cream.

ELDERBERRY (*SAMBUCUS CANADENSIS* AND *S. NIGRA*)

The native elderberry (*S. canadensis*) is a great wildlife and edible plant in the perpetual fruit garden. Its native range is from Nova Scotia and Manitoba in Canada to Georgia and Texas in the United States. The flowers and berries are edible and there are good varieties for fruit production such as 'York', 'Nova', and 'Adams'. Elderberry plants are hardy down to -40°F (-40°C).

The European elderberry (*S. nigra*) is the more ornamental of the two species and is the one most often found in garden centers. Varieties such as 'Black Lace', and 'Lemony Lace' have become popular as landscape plants. They also form berries. 'Samdal' and 'Samyak' are two good berry producers.

Elderberry plants produce best with two or more different varieties for pollination.

Elderberries are produced in midsummer to make jams, juices, and potions.

GROW

Elderberries are tough plants often found growing wild in abandoned meadows or even roadside ditches. They grow well in full to part sun, and can tolerate wet conditions, but still grow best in well-drained soil. They only require compost and mulch to grow well.

The vase-shaped shrub grows 8 to 10 feet (2.4 to 3 m) tall. Berries are best produced on one-to-three-year-old stems. In spring, prune off any stems older than three years to stimulate new growth.

Use the white or pink-colored flowers for making fritters. The black berries are used for making juice, wine, jams, and for baking. Elderberries are best eaten cooked. Raw berries can cause nausea. Birds love the berries so cover the shrub with netting once the berries start to ripen.

Elderberry fruits are favorites of birds so cover bushes with netting before fruits are ripening.

BUSH CHERRY (*PRUNUS* SP.)

If you love cherries but don't have the space for cherry trees, consider bush cherries. These were developed in Canada in the 1940s from crosses between Mongolian bush cherries and the 'Dwarf Northstar' cherry. The result is a 4 to 8-foot (1.2 to 2.4 m)-tall-and-wide shrub that produces tart cherries. These bush cherries are very hardy (down to -40°F [-40°C]), and they produce fruit sooner and sweeter than tart cherry tree varieties.

'Hansen' (*P. besseyi*) and 'Nanking' (*P. tomentosa*) bush cherries are classic 4 to 6-foot (1.2 to 1.8 m)-tall-and-wide varieties. 'Joel' and 'Joy' are dwarf bush cherries that ripen in late summer and generally are not bothered by birds. Most bush cherries need two different varieties for pollination. However, 'Carmine Jewel', 'Romeo', and 'Juliet' are newer varieties with sweeter flavor that are self-fertile.

Bush cherry shrubs are a good alternative to cherry trees if you lack space.

GROW

Plant bush cherries in full sun in well-drained soil similar to where you'd plant tree cherries. I have grown mine in an edible hedgerow mixed with other berry shrubs such as elderberry and honeyberry. Bush cherries also look great as foundation plants around a building because of their white flowers in spring. They can be planted as a windbreak and mixed with ornamental shrubs as well.

Bush cherries produce fruit a few years after planting. They do have the same issues with pests and birds as tree cherries, but because of their dwarf stature, they're easier to maintain. Cover early summer-producing bush cherries with bird netting to prevent damage. We found growing late summer-producing bush cherry varieties, such as 'Joel' and 'Joy', avoids bird damage altogether.

Harvest when the cherries are dark in color and easily come off the tree.

MULBERRY (*MORUS* SPP.)

There is no sweeter fresh fruit than the mulberry. This tree (*M. rubra*) has North American roots although there are invasive Asian (*M. alba*) varieties as well. It's hardy down to -30°F (-34°C) and low-maintenance.

The classic mulberry tree variety is 'Illinois Everbearing'. It's a good tree for cold climates. You only need one tree to get fruit, and it lives for decades. It grows 20 feet (6.1 m) tall and is a cross between a red and a white mulberry. The seed is sterile. The black fruits are produced for six weeks in summer. 'Giraldi' is a 6 to 8-foot (1.8 to 2.4 m)-tall dwarf, hybrid variety.

Mulberries are amazingly sweet summer fruits that you and the birds will love.

GROW

Plant mulberry trees on the edge of your property so they are out of the way. Dwarf varieties are nice landscape trees in a garden or mixed with other shrubs in a hedgerow or island planting.

Mulberries fruit best in full sun and well-drained soil. They need little pruning other than removing dead, diseased, and broken branches. Once established, they're hardy trees that consistently fruit each year for decades. They're great wildlife trees, feeding birds and other creatures. We share our mulberries with the birds. I cover the lower branches with a floating row cover once fruiting starts. The birds get the berries in the upper branches, and we munch on the protected berries on the lower branches. The fruits mature slowly over time, so mulberries are a great snacking tree, providing fruit most of the summer.

White mulberry (*M. alba*) trees can be invasive in some areas. They can self-sow and spread by their roots, so watch for seedlings and weed them out. Look for the native red mulberry (*M. rubra*) or hybrids with sterile seed to grow.

HARDY KIWI (*ACTINIDIA ARGUTA* AND OTHERS)

This perennial vine is not a native of North America, but I'm including it because of its usefulness in the perpetual fruit garden. It hails from Asia, is hardy down to -40°F (-40°C) and produces small kiwi fruits that look and taste like miniature versions of the fuzzy kiwi (*A. deliciosa*) except hardy kiwis have no fuzz on their skin, so they can be eaten whole.

Varieties, such as 'Anna', 'Arctic Beauty' (*A. kolomitka*), and 'Ken's Red' (*A. purpurea*) have 25-foot (7.6 m)-long vines. Most hardy kiwis need one male pollinator for every four female vines. 'Issai' is unusual in that it's self-fertile. Some varieties have colorful leaves, making them an attractive addition to the landscape. The male 'Arctic Beauty' kiwi has variegated leaves of green, white, and pink.

Hardy kiwi fruits look and taste like fuzzy kiwi. They just grow on hardier vines.

GROW

Grow hardy kiwi on a sturdy support, such as a fence, pergola, or trellis, in full sun and in well-drained, fertile soil. Hardy kiwis can get root rot and die if grown in poorly drained soil. Hardy kiwi vines like nitrogen, so amend the soil with compost annually.

Pruning is the most important chore for hardy kiwis. Prune to a strong central trunk the first year, attaching it to the support structure. Remove other shoots from the base of the plant. In subsequent years, prune the side vines down to eight to twelve buds each winter. This keeps the vines in bounds and helps stimulate fruiting.

Harvest fruits when they are fully colored and still firm. They will continue to ripen indoors after harvest.

Some areas are concerned about the invasive qualities of hardy kiwi as it can self-sow in native forests. Check your Department of Agriculture to see if it's a concern in your state.

LOWBUSH BLUEBERRY (*VACCINIUM ANGUSTIFOLIUM*) AND AMERICAN CRANBERRY (*V. MACROCARPUS*)

These two lowbush fruits are natives and delightful. However, they do require special growing environments, so I'd tackle growing these only if you're up for a challenge.

Lowbush blueberries are the ones famously found in Maine, creeping along the ground in sunny locations on rocky or sandy, acidic soils. You can grow varieties of many wild harvest lowbush blueberries in your yard, if you're willing to change your native soils. 'Brunswick' and 'Burgundy' are two good varieties. These varieties are different from dwarf blueberry varieties, such as 'Tophat', in that they only grow 12 inches (30 cm) high and creep along the ground.

Lowbush blueberries are small plants, but they produce many small berries.

The American cranberry is a staple of American Thanksgiving meals and is often seen growing in flooded bogs. However, you can create your own bog in a sunny spot with sandy, acidic soil to grow these creepers. These differ from the American cranberry bush (*Viburnum trilobum*) which is a large, native shrub that also produces red, edible berries.

GROW

Most yards won't have the right conditions for either of these creeping fruits to grow. So, you'll have to select an area, remove the existing plants, and adjust the environment to grow them.

For blueberries, you need sun, sandy soil and a pH between 4.0 and 5.0. It's best to prepare the site in fall for a spring planting. Cover the root zone of young plants with 2 inches (5 cm) of organic mulch, such as wood chips and pine needles. Fertilize with an acidifying product, such as fertilizers used for growing rhododendrons. Mow down one-half of the patch annually to stimulate new growth and better berry production.

American cranberries also like these open conditions, but they prefer a boggy soil. Dig out 10 inches (25 cm) of soil and replace it with a combination of peat moss, sand, and organic acidifying fertilizer. Fully moisten the bed. Plant American cranberry plants 2 feet (61 cm) apart and keep them well weeded. The cranberry plant runners will fill the bed in a few years, and you can expect fruit by years three or four. They don't require annual pruning.

Edible Hedegrow

CREATE AN EDIBLE HEDGEROW

An edible hedgerow uses fruiting plants to create an attractive and functional planting to block a view or define a garden. The hedgerow I'm going to describe here is 6 feet (1.8 m) wide and 30 feet (9.1 m) long and can be modified to fit your garden space. The basic idea is to grow taller fruiting plants in the back of the hedgerow with shorter, dwarf plants in the front and strawberries as a ground cover throughout.

The large plants that occupy the back of the hedgerow providing height, include two elderberry shrubs (A), an American cranberry viburnum bush (B), and two highbush blueberries (C). These plants will each grow 6 to 10 feet (1.8 to 3 m) tall when mature. That's a nice screen.

In front of these tall berry producers, plant a currant (D), a gooseberry (E), and two honeyberry bushes (F) (for adequate pollination). You can also substitute low-growing bush berry producers such as bush cherries and dwarf blueberries.

Because you're planting two-to-three-year-old shrubs in this hedgerow, planting strawberries as an understory makes sense. When I made my hedgerow, the strawberries were extras from our strawberry patch. They quickly filled in the spaces between the shrubs without competing with them for water and nutrients. We end up getting a bonus strawberry (G) crop from the hedgerow. They keep the soil healthy, weed-free, and moist for the shrubs.

Layered Fruit Tree Planting

LAYERED FRUIT TREE PLANTING

Most of my placements of fruit trees and berry shrubs are in gardens, near buildings, or in groups. But there's another technique you can try that borrows ideas from the permaculture method of gardening. This layered fruit tree planting scheme is an example of growing compatible shrubs and perennials together around a foundational fruit tree (A). The idea is that plants don't live in a vacuum. They actually grow better when growing with other plants that complement them. The fruit tree should be on the smaller side, like a dwarf plum, cherry, apple, or peach.

Around the edge of the fruit tree are low-growing, part-shade–tolerant shrubs such as gooseberry (B), currant (C), and honeyberry (D). These form a community of plants that work together to grow a strong network of roots to support one another.

Around this core group of plants are raised beds with complementary plants that fill niches in the garden. One bed might be nitrogen-fixing legumes such as peas and beans (E). Another bed might have nutrient accumulators such as comfrey and horseradish (F). These plants mine nutrients deeper in the soil and bring them up to their leaves. The leaves die back on the top of the soil, leaving their nutrients for other plants to use. In another bed, there are plants known for attracting pollinating and beneficial insects (G). Edible plants, such as lavender, borage, and lemon balm are attractive to pollinators. Finally, there's a bed that represents weed smotherers (H)—plants such as mint and strawberry that will cover the soil, preventing many weeds from growing.

While I grouped the complementary plant beds into four sections containing plants with similar roles in this illustration, you certainly can mix the different plants, based on their roles, in each bed to create a balanced system.

GROWING FRUITS IN CONTAINERS

I've mentioned in a number of places throughout this chapter the topic of growing fruits in containers. This certainly is a clever way to save space and to grow fruits where you normally can't, such as on a deck or patio.

However, container growing of any perennial requires more attention and work than in-ground growing. But once you have a system in place that works, it actually doesn't take too much extra time.

It all starts with the right fruit tree or shrub. While almost any plant can be grown in a pot with care, it's easiest to select a dwarf, self-fertile variety.

Then you'll need a pot. Generally, the larger the pot, the less work maintaining the fruit tree or shrub will be. But, of course, if this pot is to be moved to a protected site for winter, for example, then a larger pot will be more work to move. I favor the newer, rubberized plastic pots because they don't easily break and are lightweight. Some also have a self-watering mechanism and casters on the bottom.

The Soil

I've made a special heading on soil for containerized fruits because it's that important. Most potting soils contain organic material, usually in the form of peat moss; some additives

Containers can have more than one fruit growing in them, such as this fruit tree with a strawberry groundcover.

There are new varieties of raspberries and blackberries that can thrive in a container.

for good water drainage, such as perlite; and perhaps some fertilizer. While this may work for an annual plant in a pot, perennials like fruit trees need more.

A good mix to start with would be equal parts compost, perlite, and potting soil. This creates a well-drained mix that does have some nutrient- and water-holding capacity. Then add in balanced, organic, granular fertilizer (that meets the basic fertilizer needs of plants) and any special amendments based on the plants you're growing.

The Care

In my northern climate garden, I look to maximize the amount of light and heat my container fruits get. So, I place them in a microclimate in front of our south-facing garage on a gravel driveway. Watering is critical. During the heat of summer, especially on windy days, you might be watering daily. Automated watering systems using drip irrigation might be a good investment in this case. A self-watering plastic container could be another option to reduce the need for watering.

In fall in my climate, I leave the pot outdoors until freezing temperatures arrive. Usually, my deciduous plants have all dropped their leaves by then and have gone dormant. I then move the pot into an unheated garage, basement, or shed where the temperatures will stay between freezing and 40°F (4°C). No light is needed. This will keep the plants dormant until spring.

Because your tree or shrub wil live in this pot for years, it will need annual care for its roots. In late winter, I pull the pots out of their winter homes and remove the root ball. I mix up the same soil mix I used to plant with the first time. I use a saw to cut off about 2 inches (5 cm) of the root ball's circumference and bottom. This will give me new room to add fresh potting mix. It also stimulates the roots to send out side roots and grow faster. At the same time, I prune the top, reducing the branches so the roots can support the size of the tree or shrub. If your plant has weak branches or some that don't leaf out well, it may be that you haven't pruned the top enough. I then move the pot into a protected area, such as a garage, until it's warm enough to move it outside for the summer.

After learning about the many fruits you can grow in a perpetual vegetable garden, you next have to consider where they will fit in your landscape. In the next chapter, we'll dive into siting these various plants along with all the vegetables beds we've talked about in earlier chapters. I get very practical by providing five different garden designs for your continuous vegetable garden and yard.

CHAPTER 7

POWERFUL AND PRODUCTIVE PLANTING SCHEMES

I've described many of the vegetables, herbs, edible flowers, and fruits you can grow in your continuous garden. Now, it's time to talk about how to include these plants in the landscape by presenting some design options. In this chapter, I feature five different garden plans with specific details on what to grow. I talk about matching plants based on their growth characteristics, nutrient sharing, and abilities to ward off pests. I offer designs for perpetual vegetable gardens in full sun, part shade, and growing beds for a hot, summer climate. I also give a drone's-eye view of your yard, showing where fruits, berry bushes, vines, and wild edible areas can be located. All of this is to help you with the layout possibilities for growing a perpetual garden that's both attractive and productive.

FULL-SUN GARDEN PLAN

In the full-sun vegetable garden plan on the following pages, I've combined a number of techniques I've talked about in this book to grow more vegetables and herbs in less space. I include examples of vertical planting, interplanting to share space and nutrients, succession planting to grow up to three different crops in one bed during the growing season, and perennial vegetables to reduce the workload.

The illustration on the following three spreads shows six beds, each 4 x 8 feet (1.2 × 2.4 m), for a total of about 200 square feet (18.6 sq m) of planting space. The illustrations show what's growing in each bed in spring, summer, and early fall. There certainly are many other combinations you can use and replacement plants you can grow, especially if some plants succumb to the weather or pests. I also offer some growing options for each bed beyond what's illustrated. Let's take a look at each of the six beds through all three seasons.

FULL-SUN GARDEN PLAN

BED 1: Perennial Vegetable Bed. This perennial vegetable bed features two popular spring and early summer plants: asparagus (A) and strawberries (B). Asparagus is a deep-rooted vegetable, while strawberry is more shallow rooted. Because the roots are in different depths in the soil, they shouldn't compete for nutrients.

SPRING: Harvest asparagus shoots (from three-year-old plants) as they emerge for around six weeks or until the spears' diameter is less than the diameter of a pencil. Then let the spears grow into ferns. Protect strawberry flowers from spring frosts.

SUMMER: The asparagus in summer has ferns that shade the strawberries, protecting the plants from heat waves. You may need to support the ferns if they flop over. The strawberries are ripening and spreading. They create a ground cover that helps keep the soil moist, reducing the need for watering and weeding.

FALL: The asparagus ferns turn an attractive golden color and are removed in early winter to reduce the incidence of asparagus beetles and diseases. The strawberry plants overwinter in the beds and should be covered, in late fall, with straw for winter protection.

BED 2

BED 2: Warm-Season Vegetable Bed. Here we have tomato (A) and basil (B). You could use other warm-season vegetables, such as eggplants, as well.

SPRING: Plant an early-maturing cherry tomato variety, a midseason determinate variety, and a late-season heirloom variety to extend the tomato-harvest season throughout the summer. Plant tall 'Genovese' basil transplants around the tomatoes to help ward off pests such as the tomato hornworm. Seed a leafy greens mix (C) around the tomato and basil plants. The greens grow quickly while the tomatoes and basil are still small.

SUMMER: Harvest the greens until the heat or overcrowding from the tomatoes forces them to bolt. Let the greens you like self-sow and you'll get a fall crop of young plants to eat, though not as much as in spring since the warm-season plants are large by then. Start harvesting tomatoes and basil. It's better to pick a whole shoot of basil leaves instead of just individual leaves because that spurs more stem formation and bigger basil leaves later in the season. Allowing a few extra basil plants to bolt and flower is a good way to attract beneficial insects to the garden.

FALL: Continue harvesting tomatoes as they ripen before a frost and pick off the remaining basil leaves for use in the kitchen. Harvest self-sown greens (D) as needed.

FULL-SUN GARDEN PLAN

BED 3: Succession Planting. This bed is loaded with veggies that will give you multiple crops in one gardening season.

SPRING: Leave a foot or two of space at both ends of the bed for squash (A) and cucumber (B) plants. Plant Swiss chard (C) and lettuce (E) along each long edge of the bed. Sow two rows of peas (D) planted on either side of a fence placed down the center of the bed. To save space, trellis these summer squash and zucchini plants using a teepee or trellis. The elevated squash plants have less disease and insect problems and don't take over the bed.

SUMMER: The pea fence is removed and the harvested pea plants chopped and dropped for mulch. The Swiss chard continues to grow and a summer planting of bush beans (F) replaces the harvested lettuce. If one of the squash (A) or cucumber (B) plants succumb to disease or insects, plant a second crop of squash (A) or cucumbers (B) in its place. Summer-planted cucumbers and squashes often have fewer pests, grow faster due to the warm soils, and continue to produce into fall with our increasingly warm autumns.

FALL: The harvested bean plants are chopped and dropped, the other squash plant is removed if it's not doing well. A mix of carrots (E), beets (F), greens (G) and cabbage (H) transplants are planted for a fall harvest. The cucumber continues to produce.

BED 4

BED 4: Long-Season, Warm-Weather Vegetable Bed. This bed doesn't change much during the growing season and features peppers (A), along with colorful and edible flowers (B) and a cucumber (C) grown on a 45-degree, angled, cucumber trellis.

SPRING: Plant peppers, annual herbs (E), and edible flowers in part of the bed. The other section of the bed is a spring planting of cucumbers on a trellis with lettuce (D) planted beneath. The number of peppers and flowers you plant is dependent on how big an angled cucumber trellis you create.

SUMMER: Harvest the lettuce as it grows. The lettuce will mature before the cucumbers grow up the trellis and shade them. Either allow the lettuce to bolt and self-sow seeds for fall or next spring or chop and drop the healthy lettuce plants for mulch under the cucumber trellis. Harvest the edible flowers and annual herbs as needed for salads and cooking. Harvest peppers as they ripen.

FALL: The cucumbers are removed once they slow their production or insects and diseases set back the plants. In October, plant garlic cloves (F) to overwinter and be harvested next summer. Some of the annual herbs and flowers, such as calendula, dill, and cilantro, may self-sow for next spring in the bed as well.

FULL SUN GARDEN PLAN

BED 5: More Succession Planting. Kale is the mainstay in this bed. It takes advantage of the legumes fixing nitrogen to grow strong into fall.

SPRING: Plant edamame (A) along one bed edge with kale (B) transplants in the middle of the bed and bush beans (C) along the other bed edge. The length of the bean and edamame row depends on how many of these veggies you want all at once. Don't sow the whole bed length with beans or you'll have a glut of beans in summer. Leave a 3-foot (1 m) section (or larger) at the end of the bed for a block planting of carrots (D), beets (E), and radishes (F).

SUMMER: The edamame (A) is left to mature in late summer and the kale (B) continues to grow. After harvesting the early crop of roots, plant a fall crop of zucchini (G) or a bush-type winter squash such as 'Bush Delicata'. Harvest the bush bean plants and then chop and drop them for mulch. Plant a heat-tolerant lettuce (H), such as 'Summertime', in their place. The edamame (A) is left to mature in late summer and the kale (B) continues to grow. After harvesting the early crop of roots, plant a fall crop of zucchini (G) or a bush-type winter squash such as 'Bush Delicata'.

FALL: Harvest the remaining edamame plants and then chop and drop them. Plant a winter lettuce variety (I), such as 'Winter Density', in their place.

BED 6: Long-Season, Cool-Weather Vegetable Bed. This bed features cool-season vegetables that need the whole summer to mature.

SPRING: Plant cool season Brassica family crops you like the best such as Brussels sprouts (A), broccoli (C), cauliflower, and cabbage. Interplant onion (B) transplants mixed around the Brassicas. I also interplant onion (B) transplants mixed around all the *Brassicas*. The onion and kohlrabi plants usually finish producing by the time the Brussels sprout and broccoli plants get large.

SUMMER: Harvest the onions when the tops start to naturally flop. Pull the plants, allow them to cure in an airy, warm, dry location, and then cut the tops off. Harvest kohlrabi plants when the swollen bulb is 1 to 3 inches (2.5 to 7.6 cm) in diameter. Remove the whole plant and use the mild-flavored kohlrabi in salads or roasted. Harvest early cabbage and cauliflower plants as they mature. Continue harvesting broccoli side shoots throughout the season.

FALL: Harvest late-maturing cabbage varieties (i.e., 'Late Flat Dutch') and Brussels sprouts. To get your Brussels sprouts to form sprouts faster, in September, top the Brussels sprout plant so it sends more energy into the sprout formation and less into new growth.

COMPLEMENTARY ROOT SYSTEMS

This illustration shows an example of vegetables with complementary root systems growing together. Deep-rooted vegetables, such as carrots, can grow next to shallow-rooted vegetables such as lettuce and arugula. The roots occupy different zones in the soil, so they don't compete with each other for water and nutrients.

CONTAINERS

Other options to grow even more vegetables would be to use containers. Containers are great for individual plants that need heat to mature such as peppers and eggplants. They also are a great way to grow space hogs such as potatoes, sweet potatoes, and artichokes. Of course, the other advantage of containers is they can be moved to the sunniest, warmest part of your yard for better maturing in cooler climates. And to a shady afternoon location in warm climates.

Plant large vegetables, such as eggplants, in at least a 14-inch (35.6 cm) -diameter container.

This polyculture bed features leafy greens maturing around young tomatoes.

PART-SHADE GARDEN PLAN

I realize many gardeners don't have six to eight hours of full sun a day to grow their favorite vegetables and edibles. If you only have 3 to 4 hours a day, you can still grow veggies and herbs, you just have to be more selective. Root crops, greens, *Brassicas*, and some herbs will still produce, though maybe not as much as in full sun. Here are four raised beds, each 4 x 8 feet (1.2 × 2.4 m), laid out with these part-shade plants.

BED 1: Plant long-season vegetables, such as Brussels sprouts (A), broccoli (B), and cabbage (C), in the middle of the bed. Along the edges, succession plant greens, such as lettuce (D), spinach (E), and arugula (F).

BED 2: This bed has half potatoes (A) or sweet potatoes and the other half root crops. Carrots (B), beets (C), and radishes (D) are broadcast-sown in this area to save space and give you a mix of the various roots.

BED 3: This bed is for long-season greens. These are greens, such as kale (A), Swiss chard (B), and collards (C), which grow slowly into large plants that can be harvested all summer and fall.

BED 4: This is an herb and edible flower bed. Certainly, you could mix some of these plants into the other beds as well. This bed contains chives (A), cilantro (B), dill (C), parsley (D), sage (E), and thyme (F). The perennial herbs are planted along the edge of the bed. Mixed in are violas (G), mounding nasturtiums (H), and calendula (I).

HOT-CLIMATE GARDEN PLAN

Gardens everywhere are getting hotter in summer. Shade cloth can help mitigate the intensity of the heat, but growing vegetables and herbs that can take the heat will also help. In this Hot-Climate Garden planting scheme, I highlight some of the vegetables and herbs and their varieties that can thrive in the heat of summer.

BED 1: While most tomatoes (A) enjoy the summer heat, in an extreme summer climate, it's good to grow heat-tolerant varieties such as 'Heat Wave II' and 'Heat Master'. These varieties set fruit at high temperatures. Of course, mixing in basil (B) and greens (C) is an excellent way to fill the space between the tomato transplants. The basil also wards off tomato hornworms.

BED 2: Peppers (A) and eggplants (B) like the heat, so why not plant them together in one bed? Look for varieties of hot and sweet peppers that set fruit at high temperatures, such as 'Anaheim', habanero hot peppers, and 'Corno d' Toro', 'Giant Marconi', and 'Cubanelle' sweet peppers. Japanese eggplants, such as 'Ping Tung Long' and 'Orient Express', particularly can tolerate the heat. Interplant with marigolds (C) to add color and an edible flower to the bed.

BED 3: Yes, you can grow greens in a high-heat vegetable garden. It's all about selection. This bed has Mediterranean herbs, such as oregano (A), thyme (B), rosemary (C), lavender (D), and sage (E), which share space with heat-tolerant greens. These greens include New Zealand spinach (F), Swiss chard (G), amaranth (H), and collards. On the bed edge is the heat-loving malabar spinach (I) climbing up a teepee or fence.

Often the heat can affect pollination, so I highlight varieties with flowers that can set fruit in high heat. Certainly, you're welcome to grow cool-season vegetables in spring and fall, too, but I only highlight the summer vegetables here in these six, 4 x 8-foot (1.2 × 2.4 cm) raised beds.

BED 4: Southern peas, such as black-eyed peas (A), are great, heat-tolerant legumes that are easy to grow. Plant heat-tolerant, climbing, Italian heirloom tromboncino squash (B) on one side of the bed and heat-loving asparagus beans (C) on the other side, trellised up an arbor, fence, or teepee to maximize the space in the bed.

BED 5: Two standard heat-loving vegetables share a bed here. Sweet potatoes (A) and okra (B) both have many varieties that stand up well to the heat. The sweet potatoes cover the ground, conserving moisture and preventing weed growth, while the okra grows straight up and provides a bit of shade for the sweet potatoes.

BED 6: Cucumbers (A), melons (B), and watermelons (C) all thrive in the heat, but there are special varieties that can tolerate high heat. Look for 'Suyo Long', 'Ashley', and 'Armenian' cucumbers. For melons and watermelons, look for 'Hales Best' cantaloupe, casaba, and honeydew melons, 'Desert King' watermelon, and 'Crimson Sweet' watermelon.

DRONE'S-EYE VIEW OF THE PERPETUAL VEGETABLE GARDEN YARD

I've talked about the pieces of a perpetual garden and shown some of those pieces in the preceding illustrations, but I wanted to give a drone's-eye view of what your yard might look like when you put all these pieces together.

A full-sun vegetable garden occupies the sunniest spot in the backyard.

Here is an edible hedgerow that runs along the property line with your neighbor.

A part-sun veggie bed is located near the deck.

In this illustration you can see some of the possible locations to grow various fruits, herbs and wild edibles along with your main vegetable gardens. Of course these are suggestions and you should adapt your plan to your own yard.

CHAPTER 8

PLANT PROTECTION FOR SEASON EXTENSION, PEST CONTROL, AND WEATHER EXTREMES

In this book, I've covered ways to reduce your garden work and expenses by growing perennial vegetables and self-sowing vegetables, and by saving seeds and propagating your own plants. But another way to get more production with less work in the continuous vegetable garden is to protect your plants from weather conditions and pests.

Protecting young seedlings or mature plants gives you some insurance that the plants you have will survive and flourish, even when conditions are tough. When I first started vegetable gardening, I would simply plant everything over a weekend and leave to chance what would germinate, what would survive transplanting, and ultimately, what grew. Now I use plant protection on many of my plants as added insurance for success. This is especially important if you're only growing a few of many different plants where a pest or weather incident could translate to zero harvest. No tomatoes, eggplants, or melons is a sad state of affairs to face!

I now use row covers to extend the seasons in spring and fall. I use micromesh to protect rows and individual plants from pests, and we even have a polycarbonate, unheated greenhouse to really extend the growing season into winter. Let's look at some options for plant protection using a variety of materials and techniques.

ADVANTAGES OF PLANT PROTECTION

There are three main reasons to cover your plants: season extension, pest control, and weather abatement. In many situations you can use one technique or device to protect your plants in all three situations. Let's take a look at these three reasons one at a time.

SEASON EXTENSION

The primary reason a continuous vegetable gardener will cover plants is to extend the planting and harvest seasons and to enhance growth during the summer. Various covers allow you to plant weeks earlier than normal and harvest weeks later. Over the years, I've noticed with climate change that our falls are getting longer. With a little protection, I can often grow some plants into November and December in our New England garden.

Not only can you extend the season, but you also get better-quality vegetables. This is especially true of heat-loving vegetables. In our cold-climate garden, growing sweet potatoes, melons, eggplant, and other heat lovers can be a challenge, especially during cool springs and summers. Covers allow me to get young plants off to a good start and protect ripening fruits later into the fall.

PEST CONTROL

I have been an organic gardener for decades, but even with organic sprays, I still don't like spraying plants to kill harmful insects. In our continuous vegetable garden, I plant a wide variety of flowers, herbs, fruits, shrubs, and trees to create a habitat that encourages an ecological balance. By using companion planting, succession planting, crop rotation, and interplanting, I've been able to reduce the need for spraying. However, there still are some specific insects that are tough to control. That's where covers some in.

Growing a mix of vegetables, flowers, herbs, perennial flowers, shrubs, vines, and even small trees creates an ecological habitat in your garden.

Micromesh is a window screen-like material that blocks out insect pests, but allows air, water, and sun to penetrate.

Fall covers protect sensitive plants from early frost and accumulate heat for them to ripen their fruits.

There are two insects, in particular, that I've found using a season-long cover offers the best protection against. The leek moth lays eggs on onion family veggies such as leeks, onions, and garlic. The egg hatches into a green caterpillar that tunnels down the leaves toward the bulb. I notice the damage as windowpaning on the leaves, and it can even lead to damage to the bulb. I could spray Bt or Thuricide (*Bacillus thuringiensis*) on the plants repeatedly, or I can simply cover the alliums with a floating row cover or insect netting. Since no pollination is needed for alliums, I leave the covers on all season for a clean harvest.

The other pest is the Swede midge. This small, aphidlike insect attacks the growth point of cabbage family (cruciferous) veggies such as kale, broccoli, cauliflower, and Brussels sprouts. Their feeding causes the heads to be deformed and sometimes rendered unusable. It's hard to control this small insect with sprays, but again, the cruciferous vegetables don't need pollination to form the edible parts, so instead of spraying, I cover them from seedling to harvest to avoid the Swede midge. A side benefit is we don't get cabbageworms either because the adult butterfly can't lay its eggs on the cruciferous plant leaves. There are other greens, root crops, vegetables, and herbs that don't require pollination and are additional candidates for season-long insect covers. Another benefit is that rabbits, deer, and woodchucks don't seem to find these delectable vegetables as easily when they're covered.

WEATHER EXTREMES

Global warming has caused more extremes in temperature, rainfall, and catastrophic weather events. The weather seems to shift from drought to flood, sunshine to hail, and heat waves to frost warnings more quickly than I remember. This can wreak havoc on plants, especially young ones.

Plant covers can reduce physical damage to plants from hail, and winds, and heavy rains. They preserve moisture in the soil, helping mitigate drought. They can reduce leaf burn during heat waves by shading the plants.

Plants protected under covers are less bothered by the weather extremes, ensuring that more plants survive and you spend less time replanting.

WHAT VEGETABLES GROW UNDER COVERS?

Most vegetables and herbs will benefit from protection at some stage in their lives. Probably the simplest way to start using covers is with low-growing vegetables. Greens, such as spinach, arugula, lettuce, parsley, and mustard, and root crops, such as carrots, beets, radishes, turnips, and parsnips, can all grow to maturity under a low, 1 to 2-foot (30 to 61 cm)-tall row cover. A simple wire hoop, or even a support system with stakes topped with tennis balls or pots, provides enough vertical clearance for draping spun-bound, polypropylene row covers, mesh fabric, or shade cloth over the bed. Make sure the size of the fabric is wide enough to cover the bed with the added height of the hoops and that there is some extra on the ground. Secure the fabric on the ground with boards, stones, or ground stakes. Most row covers come in sizes that will fit a 3 to 4-foot (91 to 122 cm)-wide raised bed.

Of course, you can also use the low row covers in spring to cover most seedlings until they get taller. This is especially great for heat-loving veggies such as tomatoes, peppers, eggplant, beans, basil, sweet potatoes, cucumbers, melons, and squash. Remove the row covers once the weather warms, the plants start growing too tall, or they start flowering.

If you want to experiment with protecting taller vegetables and herbs that grow 3 to 4 feet (91 to 122 cm) tall, such as broccoli, onions, leeks, kale, Brussels sprouts, Swiss chard, dwarf peas, basil, and beans either all season long or in the fall, you'll need taller hoops and wider fabric pieces.

I mentioned I grow leeks, onions, and cabbage family crops under taller hoop systems primarily for pest control. We use commercial wire hoops that provide 43 inches (1.1 m) of head space in a 3-foot (91 cm)-wide bed. That's usually enough head space to grow taller vegetables under hoops all summer. I've also used PVC pipe that's cut to length for the hoops. You can purchase wider pieces of fabric to cover the taller plants or even consider buying 50-foot (1.2 m)-long commercial rolls of row cover fabric you can cut and share with other gardens. Be sure to use light, summer-weight row cover if you plan to leave it in place all season long.

If you're growing very tall vegetables or herbs, such as corn, pole beans, and indeterminate tomatoes, and want to cover them beyond the seedling stage, then you'll need a poly tunnel or greenhouse. See the sidebar on growing in these structures on page 174.

Vegetables that need cross-pollination from bees, such as tomatoes, peppers, eggplant, squash, melons, cucumbers, and pumpkins, or those that benefit from wind pollination, such as corn, can be covered to start the season, but as soon as flowering starts, the covers need to be removed.

I also have used cylinder-shaped covers on individual plants, such as hot peppers, in fall to protect the ripening existing fruits from early frosts.

Tall hoop covers allow you to grow taller vegetables to maturity under cover.

Fabric row covers come in different weights to protect plants from frost.

Clear plastic is a great row cover for heat-loving vegetables. Just make sure it's properly ventilated.

THE BEST PLANT COVERS FOR A SMALL-SPACE PERPETUAL VEGGIE GARDEN

Now that you know why you might want to cover some of your vegetables and herbs and which plants to cover, let's look at the fabric materials and frames. There has been a revolution in fabrics to protect plants over the past two decades. Clear plastic is still used in some circumstances, but spun-bound polypropylene fabrics have taken over as the go-to material for weather protection and season extension. There are also mesh materials now used for insect protection and some shading materials as well.

MATERIALS

There are a number of materials to protect plants, and I highlight the different ones in the following chart with the advantages and disadvantages of each.

Some are used to protect plants from weather and extend the season in spring and fall. Others are used to block insects and animals from attacking your plants. And some are best for mitigating hot weather in summer to extend the harvest season of cool-weather–loving plants. You can even use a combination of covers during the growing season. For example, start with spun-bound, fabric row cover in spring to get your plants started early. For those plants that like heat, replace the spun-bound fabric with slitted clear plastic to grow in summer. For those plants that don't like heat, use a lightweight micromesh material instead for insect protection. In fall, you can protect and hold mature plants in the garden well beyond the arrival of the first fall frost with heavier, weighted, spun-bound fabric row covers.

GARDEN COVERINGS

MATERIAL	DESCRIPTION	USE	ADVANTAGES AND DISADVANTAGES
Micromesh	UV-stabilized, lightweight, fine mesh fabric similar to window screen material.	Primarily used to block insects and animals from attacking your seedlings and mature plants.	It's lightweight, durable, reusable, and allows most of the sunlight through the mesh. You can see through it easily to check for insect activity. But it doesn't provide any cold weather protection.
Lightweight Spun-Bound Fabrics	Lightweight fabrics allow 85 percent of the light through, protecting plants to 28°F (-2°C).	Lightweight fabrics are used in spring or late summer to protect newly planted seed beds and young seedlings. You can grow greens and root crops to maturity under these covers as well.	Lightweight fabrics give seedlings a jump-start on the spring season while allowing enough light to shine through for their early growth. They can be used in summer to protect fall seedlings and transplants as well. However, they aren't as easy to see and water through as the micro mesh.
Medium-Weight Spun-Bound Fabrics	Medium-weight fabrics provide frost protection down to 26°F (-3°C) but allow only 70 percent of the light to shine through.	These fabrics are best used to protect plants on very cold nights in spring or fall. Because they don't allow as much light to penetrate, they are best used as a temporary fix.	Medium-weight fabrics are more durable, protect better, and are longer lasting than the lightweight ones. The thicker fabric blocks more light and makes it harder to water through. I use these mostly as fall protection from freezes to extend the season, removing them once the freeze threat is over.
Winter-Weight Spun-Bound Fabrics	Winter or heavyweight fabrics are primarily used to protect mature plants from temperatures as low as 24°F (-4°C). They block 50 percent of the light.	I use these fabrics to protect overwintering mature plants either in our garden or our unheated greenhouse.	These heavyweight covers protect plants better in fall and winter and are more durable and longer lived than lighter fabrics. But they block more light and can't be watered through.
Clear Plastic	Use 6-mil, UV-treated, polyethylene plastic for the longest life. Purchase clear plastic covers with slits in the material for ventilation. Clear plastic can also be used to cover a cold frame.	Clear plastic is great for preheating the soil in a bed before planting warm-soil–loving vegetables or early plantings of greens and root crops. Remove the plastic when planting.	Clear plastic needs more attention than other fabrics. Spring greens grow well under plastic, but the ends of the row cover need to be open for air movement. Slitted row covers help but are not as durable. Clear plastic is best used on cold frames, poly tunnels, and taller hoop tunnel systems.
Shade Cloth	This green- or black-colored, durable, knitted fabric blocks 30 to 50 percent of the light coming through but is better ventilated than a row cover. It's becoming more essential in cool summer areas experiencing more heat waves.	Shade cloth is great for protecting young seedlings in spring from heat waves, sunscald on fruiting veggies in summer, and retaining moisture in your soil during droughts. Shade cloth is also good at protecting summer-sown veggies from the heat.	Use 30 percent shade cloth for spring seedlings and the heavier 50 percent shade cloth on maturing vegetables in summer.
Cloches	These are cone-shaped covers for individual plants. They traditionally were made from glass, but now often are made from clear plastic and mesh fabrics.	Use small cloches to protect individual young plants from cold in spring or fall. Use larger cloches to protect and accelerate growth on heat-loving vegetables in summer and fall.	Small cloches have to be watched carefully and ventilated well so as not to burn developing plants. They're labor intensive this way. Fabric cloches are better at ventilating than plastic or glass. Larger cloches offer more leeway with ventilation.

Shade cloth protects young spring- or summer- sown seedlings and mature fruits from extreme heat.

Individual tall garden cloches are great for protecting specialty plants such as your favorite hot pepper.

FRAMES

There are many different framing materials you can use to support row covers or to build a tall hoop tunnel. Some come as DIY kits. What materials you use to make a frame will depend somewhat on what you're growing. Low row cover and hoop tunnel systems that only stand a few feet (about 1 m) off the ground won't need as much support as taller hoop tunnels.

For low row cover systems, 10-gauge wire, ½-inch (1 cm) PVC pipe, or even ½ to 1-inch (1 to 3 cm)-diameter wooden or metal stakes can be used to create a tunnel. The wire is most durable, especially if you purchase galvanized, corrosion-resistant wire. You can purchase wire or PVC pipe locally at home centers or hardware stores in longer pieces and cut it yourself. I have also used 2½ (76 cm)-tall wooden or metal stakes placed every few feet (about 1 m) along both edges of a raised bed. On one of my garden tours to England, I noticed gardeners at Hampton Court using clay or plastic pots set atop the stakes, over which they draped the mesh material. As mentioned previously, I've devised a similar system using old tennis balls. I slit the balls and push the slit end over the top of the stake. I find the mesh and fabric materials slide easier over the tennis balls than they do pots.

For tall hoop tunnels, purchase tall metal wire stakes. It's best if each hoop is made from two heavy-gauge wires joined by cross braces. They're easier to install and sturdier than single wire hoops.

Another option is using PVC tubing. You may want to use horizontal pieces of tubing or wood to connect PVC hoops together. This will keep them more secure during heavy winds and rain. Also, when purchasing long pieces of wire or tubing it helps to have a hoop bender. This device will help you bend the materials to more easily fit in the bed. For the PVC frame, it's also good to install pipe clamps on the raised bed and then run the cut PVC tubing through the clamps, creating a stronger tunnel.

There also is the option of purchasing freestanding frame kits with the fabric or mesh already attached. These kits are perfect for standard-sized, in-ground, or elevated raised beds. They fit over the beds and are easily secured to your structure. You can purchase these kits with spun-bound fabric, micromesh, or shade cloth. There is also a version of crop cages with chicken wire or mesh attached. These are good for protecting individual plants, such as blueberries, from birds and wildlife.

You can get creative using clay or plastic pots on a stake to prop up your row cover or netting.

Cold frames are great for growing early crops of greens, hardening off seedlings, and maturing heat-loving veggies.

It's easy to see the difference between lightweight row covers (left) and medium-weight covers (right).

You can build a cold frame inexpensively by sourcing recycled wood and old window panes.

Plastic-topped cold frames are even cheaper to build and give your plants a little extra head room.

GO TRADITIONAL WITH COLD FRAMES

Cold frames are another great way to extend the planting and harvesting window. While the technology has changed and become more sophisticated over the decades, the uses are much the same. You can sow seeds weeks before you do in the garden, harden off plants you started indoors, harvest greens and low-growing herbs early in spring and through the summer, and create succession crops so you're eating from the garden later into fall.

My first cold frame was as simple as you can get. I didn't have much money, so I went to a building salvage yard and found two matching old windowpanes and some used two-2 x 10-inch (5 × 25 cm) pieces of lumber. I created a wooden box the size of the two windows, hinged the windows side by side on the frame, and added a handle on each window. To vent the cold frame, I used a brick or piece of wood to prop the windows open. In those days, it cost me $25 to build this cold frame. Although not pretty, it worked. I've also used PVC tubing to make hoops, attached them to the wooden cold frame box with clamps, and draped clear plastic over the hoops. This allowed me to grow taller plants in the cold frame and have more leeway with temperature control.

While easy to create, managing a cold frame takes time. The air around plants can heat up quickly in spring or fall, even on a cold day. Only a few hours of overheating can kill plants. It's hard to know when—and to remember—to open or close the sashes on the cold frame. This can be compounded by not being at home all day due to work or other obligations.

One of the tricks I've used with cold frames is to err on the side of venting. Weather forecasts can be fickle, so when in doubt, open the vent in the morning, especially if you won't be home all day. Just make a note to yourself to close it in the evening during cool nights. I've also learned to place cold frames where they get a bit of afternoon shade. That can save plants from the harsh sun and reduce overheating.

Luckily, for a time-crunched, perpetual vegetable gardener, there are premade cold frame kits with automatic window vent openers. You can also just purchase the automatic vent openers and install them yourself on a homemade cold frame. Just know that most automatic openers can lift only 15 pounds (7 kg) of weight. They're best used on lightweight window sashes. This will take the guesswork out of opening and closing the cold frame and frees you to do other things.

Wire crop protection kits fit nicely over a bed protecting plants from birds and wildlife.

Poly tunnels allow you to grow tall vegetables to maturity and protect them from the elements.

The ultimate season extender is a hobby greenhouse. Good kits are expensive but they will give you years of carefree growing.

POLY TUNNEL VS. GREENHOUSE

If you have room in your yard for a larger covering system, consider building a poly high tunnel or greenhouse. This is the ultimate prize for the continuous vegetable gardener because these structures are large enough to walk inside, they protect plants from weather better than lower tunnel systems, they allow you to grow more and larger plants with less disease, and you can grow plants longer into the fall and winter. You can also use the structure for lots of other purposes, such as starting seeds, hardening off seedlings, and overwintering tender plants in pots.

If you're ready for a poly high tunnel or greenhouse, there are some considerations to keep in mind. Market growers often use a poly high tunnel simply because they're easier to install than a greenhouse, are easier to move, and, most importantly, are much less expensive. Poly high tunnel kits usually include a metal frame, greenhouse polyethylene covering, and all the accessories to build the high tunnel and gable ends. There are also DIY plans on the internet if you want to build your poly high tunnel from scratch. If you're good at building structures, you can erect your high tunnel kit in a few days to a week depending on your experience level and help.

A freestanding greenhouse is the grand prize. These also come as kits that can be built over a weekend with some help. They usually are made from sturdy metal frames and UV-protected, polycarbonate panels, and have built-in vents, windows, and doors. The advantage is obvious. You can grow in the ground or in elevated beds longer into the season. My unheated greenhouse is 9 × 12 feet (2.7 × 3.7 m). I grow in two in-ground, raised beds along the interior edges and an elevated bed. I also have four 55-gallon (208 L) barrels filled with water in the greenhouse. The water barrels accumulate heat during sunny days to release it at night, keeping the greenhouse warmer in spring and fall. In our climate, I grow figs as perennials, heat-loving tropicals, such as lemongrass and ginger, in the ground beds, and peanuts in the elevated bed. I can overwinter greens and root crops by covering the raised beds with winter-weight fabric row covers, giving the house two layers of insulation.

The winter-weight row cover provides added protection inside the polycarbonate greenhouse.

Put hardware mesh netting around the base of the greenhouse when constructing it to keep mice and voles from tunneling under the structure and making a winter home inside.

The ground stays thawed, and the crown and stems are protected from freezing. This also extends the harvest season of tender vegetables well into winter most years.

You can grow a wide variety of plants, even tropicals, in a greenhouse.

In the coming final chapter, let's go even further with your continuous vegetable garden by taking it indoors. The ultimate ideal is to have twelve months of vegetables and herbs for eating and cooking. In warm winter climates that's possible, but even in a cold climate, indoor gardening can extend the edible season. Let's look at some ideas for how to grow vegetables indoors, even in winter.

CHAPTER 9

BRINGING PERPETUITY INDOORS

Hopefully you've gotten a good sense of how to grow a perpetual or continuous vegetable garden that also includes herbs, edible flowers, and fruits outdoors in your yard. If you're still hungry for more and want to extend your growing season longer, you can grow food indoors as well.

In this chapter, we'll discuss which harvested vegetables are easiest to store indoors for eating in winter. I won't be covering canning, freezing, and preserving food; that information is readily available in many food preservation books and online. Instead, I will talk about the easiest harvested vegetables to save and how to make them last the longest indoors and occupy the least amount of space.

I'll also discuss bringing potted herbs and even some potted vegetable plants indoors to continue growing in a sunny window, under grow lights, or to hold in dormancy until spring. I've had good success growing herbs, such as chives, mint, and parsley, and some vegetables, such as peppers, indoors. Even if only for a while, it's nice to have that fresh taste of summer in winter meals.

Finally, for those who want to grow further, you'll learn about growing microgreens and baby greens indoors under lights to have these plants all winter long.

A basement can be an ideal place to store vegetables in winter but not the only place.

Storage racks are a great investment to store many vegetables including potatoes.

STORING VEGETABLES INDOORS

The two keys to storing harvested vegetables indoors for eating in winter are having the right location for them and choosing the easiest vegetables to store. Most harvested storage vegetables need a cool, dark place to spend the winter. Having the right temperature ensures they will last a long time in storage. However, even if you don't have the exact ideal temperatures I'll mention for each vegetable, you still can store them. They just may not last until spring and will need to be consumed faster.

While you can store many harvested vegetables indoors under the right conditions, there are certain ones I've found to be easier. Garlic, shallots, dried beans, onions, potatoes, sweet potatoes, 'Long Keeper' tomatoes, and small winter squash are simple and easy to store without taking up a lot of space. Always store the best quality, undamaged seeds, tubers, bulbs, and fruits. Certainly, carrots, beets, cabbages, turnips, pumpkins, and other veggies could be stored all winter, too, but they need either more climate control than I'm willing to invest in (i.e., a root cellar) or they need more space than I have available in our basement. I do store some veggies, such as carrots, beets, radicchio, and cabbage, in the ground in our garden under row covers until it gets too cold, and then I keep them in our refrigerator after harvest, and for a few weeks beyond that. But of course, you need to have a good-sized refrigerator to do that. The easiest vegetables to store are the ones that do well in cool and dry conditions such as in a refrigerator or basement. Here's a chart of how to store those easy-to-keep vegetables.

WINTER STORAGE CONDITIONS

VEGETABLE	IDEAL STORAGE TEMPERATURE	HOW TO STORE	LENGTH OF STORAGE TIME
Beans	Room temperature (70°F [21°C])	It's important to harvest your dried beans when they are completely mature. If frost threatens, remove the plants and continue letting them dry in a well-ventilated room. Dried beans should be their mature color and hard so you can't dent the bean with your fingernail. If not completely dry, they could get moldy in storage. Once dry, store in a sealed, glass jar in a cool, dark location.	One year
Garlic and Shallots	32°F to 40°F (0°C to 4°C)	Store garlic and shallots in a cool, dark location with good air circulation. Braid and hang softneck garlic. Don't hang braided garlic in the kitchen unless you'll be using it soon. I've found placing a clay pot over garlic bulbs helps the bulbs last longer in storage.	Hardneck garlic lasts 3 to 4 months in storage if you keep the temperatures closer to freezing. Softneck garlic lasts six months.
Onions	35°F to 45°F (2°C to 7°C)	Let onions cure in a well-ventilated, warm room (70°F [21°C]) for two weeks until the outer skins become dry. Store in mesh bags or a well-ventilated boxes or racks in a cool, dark location.	Grow long day onion varieties, such as 'Cortland' and 'Blush', for the best storage. These varieties can last up to six months in storage. Other onion varieties last 3 to 4 months.
Potatoes	40°F to 50°F (4°C to 10°C)	Cure potatoes in a well-ventilated, 60°F (16°C) location for two weeks to allow the skins to toughen. Store in a dark room to prevent the skins from turning green. Store in a well-ventilated room in perforated boxes or perforated plastic bags.	Good storage potato varieties, such as 'Yukon Gold', and 'Burbank Russet', can last six months in storage. Other varieties last 3 to 4 months.
Sweet Potatoes	55°F to 60°F (13°C to 16°C)	Cure sweet potato tubers after harvest in a well-ventilated, warm (80°F [27°C]) room for one week to heal small cuts and allow the starches to turn into sugars. Store in a dark, well-ventilated room in perforated boxes.	Four to five months
Tomatoes	55°F to 65°F (13°C to 18°C)	Harvest fully or partially ripe, clean fruits. Wrap in newspaper and keep out of direct sunlight in a warm room. Once fully ripe, move to a cool room.	The key to storing ripe tomatoes for months is variety selection. 'Longkeeper', 'Garden Peach', and the 'Pomodoro d'Inverno' (see sidebar) last the longest. If blemish-free and not touching other tomatoes, these fruits can last for 4 to 6 months in storage.
Winter Squash	50°F to 55°F (10°C to 13°C)	Harvest winter squash when the skin is thick and can't be nicked by pressing your thumbnail on the skin. Cure winter squash (except acorn) for a week at 70°F to 80°F (21°C to 27°C). Store in a cool, dark, dry room.	Three to six months, depending on the variety. For longest storage, try butternut and hubbard squashes.

Braid and hang soft-neck garlic for off-season use in the kitchen.

ITALIAN WINTER STORAGE TOMATOES

From the hills of southern Italy comes an interesting group of tomatoes that are known for their long-storage life as fresh tomatoes. 'Pomodora d'Inverno' or "winter tomatoes" are small-fruited, red or yellow selections harvested in fall, strung in clusters, and hung indoors for winter use. Varieties such as 'Piennolo Giallo' and 'Piennolo Rossa' are from the Naples, Italy, area. These are small, red- or yellow-fruited cherry tomatoes with a small nipple on the bottom. The fruits have low water content, making them good for long-term storage. Trusses of fruits are harvested and looped together into a ristra (strung-up bunch) and hung in Italian kitchens. Supposedly, they can last up to 4 to 6 months as fresh tomatoes.

These varieties are now available in the United States, and I plan on trying some soon.

Italian heirloom winter tomatoes hung in a ristra can store for months indoors.

BRINGING IN POTTED VEGGIES AND HERBS

Another way to have the fresh flavor of summer vegetables and herbs in winter is to literally bring whole plants indoors. Now, you're probably not going to bring a mature, large squash or tomato plant (I talked about overwintering a live tomato plant indoors in chapter 5) indoors. But there are other vegetables and herbs that are much easier to bring inside and fit in your home. Many herbs and some vegetables can stay productive indoors, and I'm highlighting the easiest of them to try.

HERBS INDOORS

For herbs, I would start with the Mediterranean plants. Low-growing herbs, such as thyme and oregano, and taller Mediterranean herbs, such as rosemary, lavender, and sage, all can overwinter as whole plants indoors. They stay a manageable size in pots, can take the cooler temperatures indoors in winter, and, if given enough light, can stay productive into the winter.

The keys to growing these sun-loving herbs are a sunny window or grow lights, and well-drained soils. For example, I grow rosemary in a west-facing window, and it grows fine, even with our sometimes weeks of cloudy, cold weather in winter. I find the soil has to be well-drained and kept moist, but on the dry side. That means I water less frequently, but thoroughly in winter. If the soil stays too wet, the leaves will drop. If too dry, the leaves will shrivel and die.

Other herbs like a bit more water and can take less light. Parsley and chives are good examples. I often take a few of both plants indoors in winter. Parsley is a biennial, so I know that come spring it will send up a flower stalk and harvests will be finished. Consequently, I use the leaves in cooking all winter with the idea that the plant will be composted in spring. Parsley likes moisture, and it's easy to know if your parsley plant is happy. If the leaves droop, water it.

Chives are even easier. They're perennials and will continue to put out new growth in winter. I often cut mine back to the soil level and let new flushes of young, tender leaves emerge for cooking. Come spring, the plant goes back into the garden.

Many herbs can overwinter in a sunny window indoors for use in the kitchen.

Parsley is a good plant to overwinter. Keep harvesting the leaves all winter and in spring, just compost it.

If you have a very sunny window or grow lights, you can keep a pepper plant growing indoors until spring.

High-intensity grow lights can even allow you to mature tomatoes indoors in winter.

VEGETABLES INDOORS

There are a number of vegetables you can bring indoors to "finish" inside in fall and winter. Certainly, leafy greens, such as lettuce and spinach, can be brought inside. But I'd rather use the space growing baby greens under lights and have them all winter, instead of finding room for a mature lettuce head that will last just a few weeks.

If you have space, try some special vegetables. Dwarf tomatoes and peppers are good candidates for indoor growing. Dwarf indeterminate tomato varieties, such as 'Tidy Treats', are less than 2 feet (61 cm) tall, fit in a pot, tray, or bench easily, and produce tasty fruits. Their indeterminate nature means they keep fruiting. You can even grow smaller versions, such as 'Tiny Tim' and 'Red Velvet', but they may stop producing in winter due to their determinate nature. I like these small-fruited varieties because they take up less room than larger, big-fruited varieties, and they are more productive.

Whole pepper plants are another good choice for bringing indoors in fall. In chapter 5, I talk about overwintering them. You can also keep pepper plants growing indoors with supplemental lighting. I like the smaller-fruited varieties, such as the 'Lunchbox' peppers, and hot peppers for bringing indoors.

With both tomatoes and peppers, quarantine the plants before moving them totally indoors and scout them for pests. Peppers, in particular, can carry lots of aphid eggs indoors that hatch into an infestation in winter without predators around. Spray with insecticidal soap or neem oil to control them.

Mature tomatoes and peppers may continue producing in a sunny window indoors for a few months in fall, depending on your climate and sun exposure. But eventually, in most places, they will need supplemental light to survive and keep producing in winter.

Having a light setup makes success a much greater possibility. Tomatoes and peppers need full-spectrum, high-intensity lighting to keep fruiting. The most cost-efficient lighting would be using full-spectrum LED lights. Place these lights 12 inches (30 cm) above your tomato and pepper

For quick fresh greens, grow sprouts in a jar.

plants on a bench or tray and run them twelve to sixteen hours a day. Use a heating mat under the pots to help keep the soil warm. Of course, keep the air consistently warm with no cold drafts.

To keep tomatoes and peppers fruiting in winter, you'll also need to play honeybee. Normally, wind and insects pollinate these vegetables, but indoors you'll have to be the bee. When the flowers open in the morning, use a cotton swab, artist's paintbrush, or even an electric toothbrush to shake the flowers and to pollinate them. Use a well-drained potting mix, water the soil when dry, and fertilize regularly with a liquid organic fertilizer. The plants may slow in production, even with the supplemental light during the depths of winter, but they shouldn't go dormant.

SPROUTS, MICROGREENS, AND BABY GREENS

If you really want to grow some of your own food in winter, then greens may be the answer. Unlike fruiting vegetables like tomatoes and peppers, greens don't need as much light to produce their edible parts. They are quick maturing and can be succession planted right through winter. The differences in growing various greens are their age at harvest. Let's start with sprouts.

GROWING SPROUTS

Sprouts are seeds that have just germinated. They're eaten when still in the cotyledon (baby leaf) stage of growth. This means they're quick to grow.

Many plants, such as alfalfa, broccoli, clover, radish, peas, and sunflowers, can be sprouted to eat. Sprouts are simple to grow. You can purchase sprouting trays or simply use a glass jar. Sprouting trays allow for better airflow and less risk of mold.

In a quart-sized Mason jar with a mesh lid, soak 1 to 2 tablespoons (10 to 20 g) of seeds overnight. Twice daily, rinse the seeds with fresh water. Leave the jar in a dark room out of direct sunlight until the seeds start germinating. Then bring the jar into a bright room to green up. Depending on the seeds, within seven to ten days, you'll have sprouts to eat.

MICROGREENS

Microgreens are probably the simplest way to grow greens indoors. Microgreens are a wide variety of vegetables and herbs that are harvested while the plants are very small. They are more than just common leafy greens such as lettuce, arugula, and spinach. Microgreen mixes may also contain beets, kale, basil, radish, peas, bok choi, and even sunflowers. All you need to do is to grow these seedlings until the first true leaves form and then harvest. This means after only one to two weeks, you could be harvesting microgreens.

The setup for microgreens is easy. You'll only need a sunny window, seed trays, potting soil, and seeds. That's it! Select a window that gets at least four hours of sunshine a day. In darker homes, consider using a grow light setup. More on that in a minute.

Any shallow tray would be perfect to use for growing microgreens. A seed-starting tray is fine, as well as plastic trays or containers from the grocery store. They don't need drainage holes. Select a lightweight, seed-starter soil to grow in. You can make your own microgreen seed mixes or buy premixed seed packets online or at the garden center.

STEPS TO GROWING MICROGREENS

Here are the steps to growing your microgreens:

1. Fill the seed starting tray with 2 inches (5 cm) of seed-starting potting soil.
2. Water until the soil is as damp as a wrung-out sponge.
3. Broadcast the seed on the top of the soil, trying to spread it evenly across the tray.
4. Sprinkle a thin layer of more soil over the seed and gently press the soil with your hands.
5. Mist the seed tray daily to keep the soil moist. You can also cover the seed tray with plastic to conserve moisture. But check it daily. Once the seeds start germinating, remove the cover.
6. Once the seedlings' first true leaves form, begin cutting the seedlings at the soil line with scissors to harvest.
7. Rinse and eat or store them. Microgreens will last up to ten days in the refrigerator.
8. Sow trays continuously to have microgreens throughout the winter.

A seed-starting light setup is ideal for growing microgreens indoors.

Harvest microgreens with scissors once the true leaves form.

Baby greens will regrow after harvest if you don't cut them right at the ground level.

GROWING BABY GREENS

If you want to grow more greens indoors, create an indoor growing setup to grow baby greens. The difference between microgreens and baby greens is age. The baby greens are allowed to grow for about three weeks, until the true leaves are about 4 inches (10 cm) long. Of course, the harvest timing also depends on your need for greens in the kitchen.

The best greens to grow to the baby stage include lettuce, spinach, arugula, kale, and Swiss chard. Loose leaf lettuces, such as 'Baby Oakleaf', 'Tom Thumb', and 'Black-Seeded Simpson', are the quickest lettuces to grow.

Baby greens will most likely need grow lights to grow their best. Even in a full-sun, south-facing window, the plants won't have enough light. Since you're eating just the leaves, a simple, two-bulb grow light system would be fine for microgreens and baby greens. Select one cool-white fluorescent tube and one warm-white fluorescent tube. You can also use compact, full-spectrum fluorescent tubes, such as T-5 bulbs, which give your plants a broader light spectrum, or LED lights. Run the lights fourteen hours per day.

Unlike microgreens, you'll need deeper containers to grow baby greens. The soil should be at least 4 inches (10 cm) deep. Deep seed-starting trays, window boxes, or any other deep, plastic containers work fine as long as they have drainage holes. You can also use trays with bottom-watering reservoirs that keep the soil evenly moist and are less work. Some tray systems also have a clear plastic dome lid, which keeps the soil moist and temperatures in the ideal 65°F to 70°F (18°C to 21°C) range for germination.

Use lightweight, moistened potting soil and broadcast-sow the seeds. Remove the domed lid once the greens start germinating to prevent rot and increase air circulation. Set the lights a few inches (about 8 cm) above the emerging plants and raise the lights higher as the plants grow. Keep the soil moist. Fertilize lightly with liquid fertilizer.

Harvest baby greens about twenty days after sowing. Unlike microgreens, baby greens can regrow for a second crop. Cut the leaves higher with a pair of scissors, and do not remove or damage the growth point in the middle of the plant. Harvest only as much as you need for that day. The greens will stay fresher growing in the soil than cut and stored in the refrigerator. Plant a new crop every two to three weeks to have a continuous supply in winter.

WRAP UP

This puts the finishing touches on the technique of Continuous Vegetable Gardening. As you've read, this garden looks and feels familiar but has many twists. Its goal is to produce a steady supply of food throughout the growing season, and perhaps beyond, while requiring less work, less money, and generally, fewer inputs from you. Although lower maintenance, by nature, this garden does need *you*. Even spending five to ten minutes a day looking around and engaging in your garden will benefit you and the plants growing there. You'll feel more relaxed, and your garden will have fewer problems and produce more food and fun. Even if you use only a few of the ideas found in these pages, you'll be well on your way to a productive continuous vegetable garden.

RESOURCES

Here are some helpful books and websites about fruit growing and vegetable gardening:

AHS Essential Guide to Organic Vegetable Gardening by American Horticultural Society (Cool Springs Press, 2025)

The Complete Guide to No-Dig Gardening by Charlie Nardozzi (Cool Springs Press, 2020)

Edible Perennial Gardening: Growing Successful Polycultures in Small Spaces by Anni Kelsey (Chelsea Green, 2019)

Grow Fruit Trees Fast: A Beginner's Guide to a Healthy Harvest in Record Time by Susan Polzner (Orchard People, 2022)

Grow Your Own Mini Fruit Garden: Planting and Tending Small Fruit Trees and Berries in Gardens and Containers by Christy Wilhelmi (Cool Springs Press, 2021)

Growing Perennial Foods: A Field Guide to Raising Resilient Herbs, Fruits, and Vegetables by Acadia Tucker (Stone Pier Press, 2019)

Growing Under Cover: Techniques for a More Productive, Weather-Resistant, Pest-Free Vegetable Garden by Niki Jabbour (Storey Books, 2020)

Plant Partners: Science-Based Companion Planting Strategies for the Vegetable Garden by Jessica Walliser (Storey Books, 2020)

The Vegetable Garden Problem Solver Handbook by Susan Mulvihll (Cool Springs Press, 2023)

The Vegetable Gardening Book by Joe Lamp'l (Cool Springs Press 2022)

A Step-by-Step Guide for Growing Microgreens at Home. A Pennsylvania State University Extension site for all the basics of growing microgreens at home. *extension.psu.edu/a-step-by-step-guide-for-growing-microgreens-at-home*

ATTRA-Sustainable Agriculture Season Extension. Good website for all types of season extension. Although geared toward a market gardener, you'll be able to find some good tips here. *attra.ncat.org/topics/season-extension*

Bushel and Berry. This commercial website has many varieties of dwarf berry plants and their growing information. *bushelandberry.com*

Charles Dowding. You'll find articles, videos, and a YouTube channel about no-dig gardening in the UK. *charlesdowding.co.uk*

Charlie Nardozzi. This site includes articles, podcasts, videos, a YouTube channel, and webinars by the author. *gardeningwithcharlie.com*

Joe Lamp'l. This gardening TV series has associated podcasts, videos, and classes. *growingagreenerworld.com*

Morag Gamble. Learn about permaculture and no-dig gardening information and classes. Based in Australia. *ourpermaculturelife.com*

Savvy Gardening. Online courses, articles, videos, and books. *savvygardening.com*

Seed Saver's Exchange Education and Events. The site has information on seed saving for home gardeners. Includes vegetable seed sources. *seedsavers.org/learn/seed-saving*

Soil Food Web. Dr. Elaine Ingham, founder, presents information, webinars, and classes on building healthy soils. *soilfoodweb.com*

USDA National Agricultural Library. This site includes garden guides, articles, and books on vegetable gardening. *www.nal.usda.gov/plant-production-gardening/vegetable-gardening*

ABOUT THE AUTHOR

Charlie Nardozzi is a nationally-recognized and Regional Emmy® Award-winning garden writer and speaker, and radio, television, and online personality. He has worked for more than thirty-five years bringing expert gardening information to home gardeners. Charlie delights in making gardening information simple, easy, fun, and accessible to everyone.

Charlie's energy, exuberance, and love of the natural world makes him a dynamic public speaker and presenter. He has spoken at national venues such as the Northwest Flower and Garden Show, Philadelphia Flower Show, Canada Blooms Flower Festival, Colonial Williamsburg Gardening Symposium, and master gardener conferences, trade shows, and garden club meetings across North America.

If you can't hear him speak in person, consider attending or purchasing one of his webinars at GardeningwithCharlie.com. Charlie has authored eight gardening books, has two radio shows in New England, and hosts a TV show in his home state of Vermont. He's the former host of PBS's *Garden Smart*, reaching more than 60 million households. He's also a consultant for companies and organizations such as Velcro.com, Gardeners Supply Company, and Vermont Public promoting gardening for kids and seniors.

Charlie leads garden and food tours in Europe and the Americas, including locations such as Sardinia, Sicily; the Lake District of Italy; Provence, France; Portugal; the Chelsea Flower Show in England; Cuba; Denmark; and Sweden.

ACKNOWLEDGMENTS

Vegetable gardening is in my blood. I'd like to first thank my family. When I was growing up, I was surrounded by my grandparent's farm. Vegetables, herbs, and fruits were always available to cook and eat. And thanks to my present family, especially my wife, Wendy, for enjoying all my experimentation with different gardening techniques and edibles. The techniques may not have always worked and the trial vegetables and fruits didn't always taste great, but there has never been a dull summer in our garden.

For this book, I especially want to thank Jessica Walliser at Cool Springs Press. She started the conversation with me about writing another edible gardening book. I enjoyed our back-and-forth process, finally landing on the continuous vegetable gardener topic. Jessica is a great communicator and easy to work with. Plus, her experience with vegetable gardening guided this book and offered some of the unique techniques that you see in these pages. Special thanks goes to Gabrielle Bethancourt-Hughes for guiding the editorial process, and keeping me on track with deadlines and details. Thanks also to Aime Sund for her copyediting skills and inquisitiveness about the gardening world, and to Kerri Landis for her proofreading prowess. Thanks to art director Kelly Desabrais for guiding the book creatively, and many thanks to Mattie Wells for her wonderful design and illustrations. She did an excellent job making the garden plans come to life and be easy to follow. And thanks to Steve Roth for helping market the book, and to all the other members of the Cool Springs Press team.

INDEX

www.ingramcontent.com/pod-product-compliance
Lightning Source LLC
LaVergne TN
LVHW070530260326
834485LV00008B/9

* 9 7 8 0 7 6 0 3 9 8 7 6 0 *